Fear Not!

Preaching
IN THE
Year of Luke

Bill East

Fear Not!

Preaching

IN THE

Year of Luke

DOMINICAN PUBLICATIONS

First published (2009) by
Dominican Publications
42 Parnell Square
Dublin 1

ISBN 1-905604-11-4
978-1-905604-11-1

British Library Cataloguing in Publications Data.
A catalogue record for this book is available
from the British Library.

Cover design by Bill Bolger

Printed in Ireland by
ColourBooks Ltd
Baldoyle, Dublin 13

Contents

Advent	7
The Season of Christmas	15
Lent	25
Paschal Triduum	36
The Season of Easter	40
Solemnities of the Lord	59
The Ordinary Sundays of the Year	63

Advent

First Sunday of Advent
ADVENT

Readings
Jer 33:14-16; 1 Thess 3:12–4:2; Lk 21:25-28.34-36

Advent is my favourite time of the year. We look forward to celebrating the birth of our Saviour at Christmas; look forward also to his final coming on the clouds with power and great glory, as promised in today's Gospel. The season itself is enhanced by some of the finest hymns ever written, some of them, alas! not as well known as they should be in the Catholic Church: *Wake, O Wake! with Tidings Thrilling; Lo, He Comes with Clouds Descending; On Jordan's Bank; O Come, O Come Emmanuel.*

A pity though, you might think, to start the season of Advent with the chilling message Jesus gives to his disciples: 'There will be signs in the sun and the moon and stars, on earth nations in agony ... men dying of fear as they await what menaces the world.' Who could possibly look forward with pleasure to such a catastrophe?

The message is of a piece with the entire Chrisian Gospel. Christ is risen, ascended, glorified: but first he had to be crucified. Saint Paul tells us that Jesus, 'for the sake of the joy which lay in the future endured the cross, disregarding the shamefulness of it all.' Nevertheless the agony and shame of the cross had to be endured before Jesus attained that joy which lay in the future. So it is with us: we cannot look for resurrection unless we are prepared to endure the crucifixion. Jesus tells us that unless we take up our cross and follow him to Calvary, we cannot continue on the journey with him to the joys of heaven.

Jesus will not enlist us as his disciples under false pretences. He warns us, on this very first day of the Church's year, of agony and menaces and fear ahead. All the same, the emphasis of today's message is one of hope, hope of glory to come. When these disasters occur, we are to hold our heads high, for our liberation is near at hand.

What is true on the cosmic level is also true on the more ordinary level of our daily lives. Many terrible things happen in our lives: sickness and pain, bereavement and grief, guilt and shame. There are times when, even if the powers of heaven are not shaken, our own world is most certainly shaken, and seems to be falling down around our ears.

At these times we must remind ourselves that our personal way of the cross does not end at Calvary, though it certainly passes through that dreadful place, but leads to glory. We may walk through the valley of the shadow of death, but our Good Shepherd has been that way before, and will lead us through that dark valley to green pastures and still waters, and surround us with goodness and kindness all the days of our life.

Second Sunday of Advent
JOHN DONNE'S POEM

Readings Bar 5:1-9; Phil 1:3-6.8-11; Lk 3:1-6

I wonder if you know John Donne's fine poem, 'At the round earths imagin'd corners blow.' He writes of the angels blowing the last trumpet, and the dead rising from their graves:

> At the round earths imagin'd corners, blow
> Your trumpets, Angells, and arise, arise
> From death, you numberlesse infinities
> Of soules, and to your scattred bodies goe,

He lists all the ways these people may have died, whether through Noah's flood at the beginning of creation, or through the fire that will burn up the world at its end, or old age, accident, war, sickness or whatever cause:

> All whom the flood did, and fire shall o'erthrow,
> All whom warre, dearth, age, agues, tyrannnies,
> Despaire, law, chance, hath slaine.

He mentions too those, who, according to Saint Paul, will still be alive at the last trumpet:

> and you whose eyes,
> Shall behold God, and never tast deaths woe.

But then, like so many poets when they reach the ninth line of their sonnet, he has second thoughts. Perhaps after all it would be better to delay the last judgement; Donne is not yet ready for it:

> But let them sleepe, Lord, and mee mourne a space,
> For, if above all these, my sinnes abound,
> 'Tis late to aske abundance of thy grace,
> When wee are there; here on this lowly ground,
> Teach me how to repent; for that's as good
> As if thou hadst seal'd my pardon, with thy blood.

Donne expresses a dilemma in which we often find ourselves. 'Come, Lord Jesus, come soon', we pray; but do we really want him to come *that* soon? Would we rather not carry on as we are at least for the time being? What is the right balance between, on the one hand, the legitimate enjoyment of the good things of this world, human love, affection between man and wife, parent and child, friend and friend, and on the other, the desire so often expressed in the New Testament that these things will soon come to an end and be replaced with the kingdom of Christ?

An excellent balance is struck, it seems to me, in our letter of Saint Paul to the Philippians. Saint Paul, more than anybody, was committed to the coming of Christ. He refers a couple of times, in a short passage, to the Day of Christ, by which he means the day when Christ will come in glory as King and Judge of All. But what we get mostly from this passage is Paul's idea of how we should spend the intervening time. Life on earth, for Paul, is a process of never-ending improvement, of growing more and more like Christ.

If we look at the words of Saint Paul we shall see what I mean by 'never-ending.' 'My prayer is that your love for each other may increase more and more, and never stop improving your knowledge and deepening your perception so that you can always recognise what is best.' He doesn't say to *do* what is best or to *be* what is best, simply to *recognise* what is best. This is only a stage on the way.

Then he goes on, 'This will help you to become pure and blameless.' You might think that what you'd done already would have made you pure and blameless, but there is still more to do. He goes on further, 'and prepare you for the day of Christ' – you might have thought that being pure and blameless would be adequate preparation for the day of Christ, but always in Paul there is more to come – 'for the day of Christ, when you will reach the perfect goodness which Jesus Christ produces in us for the glory and praise of God.'

Absolute perfection will only be reached in Christ, on the day of Christ, but there is a lot we can do, and have to do, in preparation for that great day. Every day offers us the opportunity to make progress towards that goal: to increase our love for each other, to strengthen those bonds of love between husband and wife, parent and child, friend and friend. Every day of this life is a precious gift of God, offering us opportunities for acts of kindness, love, self-denial, generosity, which will help to prepare a way for the Lord, to make his paths straight; which will help to fill in those valleys of despair, depression and misery, and lay low those mountains of pride and arrogance, and so prepare for that day of Christ, when all shall see the salvation of God.

Third Sunday of Advent
REJOICE!

Readings Zeph 3:14-18; Phil 4:4-7; Lk 3:10-18

I've never been keen on having my photograph taken, because the photographer always tells me to smile. I flatter myself that I can smile as well as anyone, but I've never found it easy to smile to order. Tell me to smile, and my face freezes. You may feel the same about being told to rejoice. Tell people to rejoice, and immediately they think of a thousand reasons to be miserable.

And yet our Mass today does tell us to rejoice, right from the beginning, right from the Entrance Antiphon: 'Rejoice in the Lord always; again I say, rejoice!' That Entrance Antiphon is very ancient. The Latin of which it is a translation runs: '*Gaudete in Domino semper: iterum dico, gaudete.*' It gives its name to this Sunday: *Gaudete* Sunday, the Sunday to rejoice. We have the Scripture reading from which the antiphon is taken. In the ap-palling translation which we are constrained to use, 'I want you to be happy, always happy in the Lord; I repeat, what I want is your happiness.' But in a more literate translation, 'Rejoice in the Lord always; again I say, rejoice!'

But *do* we rejoice? It is far easier to grumble than to rejoice, to be miserable rather than to be happy. How many conversations have we had lamenting the poor state of affairs in the world: the drivel on the television, the bad manners of the young, the dis-turbing levels of crime. Do we take the same pleasure in talking about all the wonderful things in the world: the excellent music to hear, the beautiful pictures to see, the challenging books to read, the food, so plentiful and varied, the flowers, the sunsets; or for that matter, the thousands of kind and wise and interest-ing people we meet?

When did you last have a really good rejoice? At the birth of your children, perhaps, or at the news of the birth of a grand-child? Do we lead fairly miserable lives, punctuated by occasional bouts of rejoicing? 'Rejoice in the Lord always', says Saint Paul. Not, rejoice in the Lord occasionally, or rejoice in the Lord once in a blue moon, but rejoice in the Lord always. That's all very well for Saint Paul to say, you might think, but he didn't have to put up with what I have to put up with.

Didn't he, though? He talks in one place about some of the things he did have to put up with. 'Five times I have received at the hands of the Jews the forty lashes less one. Three times I have been beaten with rods; once I was stoned. Three times I have been shipwrecked; a night and a day I have been adrift at sea; on frequent journeys, in danger from rivers, danger from robbers, danger from my own people, danger from Gentiles, danger in the city, danger in the wilderness, danger at sea, danger from false brethren; in toil and hardship, through many a sleepless night, in hunger and thirst, often without food, in cold and exposure. And apart from other things, there is the daily pressure upon me of my anxiety for all the churches.'

How does that compare with what you have to put up with? But in spite of all that, Saint Paul says, 'Rejoice in the Lord always'.

Fourth Sunday of Advent
VISITATION

Readings Mic 5:1-4; Heb 10:5-10; Lk 1:39-44

I have somewhere a picture of the Visitation, a reproduction from some medieval manuscript. It's a familiar icon or holy picture throughout the Church: two women embracing, their gestures indicating mutual support and love. Even if you do not own such a picture, you have probably imagined the scene often enough in your mind's eye, because the Visitation is one of the mysteries of the Rosary, which I suppose most of us contemplate from time to time.

Two women, Mary and Elizabeth: a very little group. As small, in fact, as a group can be; any fewer, and there wouldn't be a group at all. And yet that picture is an image of the whole Church. Everything essential to the Church, what it is and what it does, is contained in that picture. Christ is present, in the womb of Mary, and of course God is in Christ, reconciling the world to himself. Christ's prophet and fore-runner John is present there, already acknowledging the coming of one greater than himself, heralding his coming by leaping in his mother's womb. The women are praising and worshipping their Saviour and their God. Mary is about to break forth into her great prophetic song, the *Magnificat*, praising God's mighty works in all ages. She is also, on a more human level, visiting a friend and kinswoman, ministering to her material needs. The whole mystery of salvation is present in that scene: Christ our God, enthroned in his mother's womb, the prophets announcing his coming, his followers offering due glory and worship to God and fellowship and support to one another.

Likewise the whole mystery of salvation is present in countless scenes all over the world, wherever two or three people gather together in Christ's name. Wherever a mother prays with her children, wherever two friends meet to say the Rosary, wherever husband and wife say their prayers together, something wonderful is happening, something more than merely human. Christ himself is present in that group – he promises us as much himself. Christ our God stands among his faithful, accepting their worship, granting their requests. Do we always realise this? Do we take a proper view of our family prayers?

Another picture comes into my mind. It's called *The Angelus*. A man and a woman – presumably a man and his wife – are standing in a hayfield. They are pausing from their labours for a moment, resting on their pitchforks. From a distant church we can imagine the sound of the Angelus bell. Their heads are bowed in prayer. The picture is about the sanctification of our daily work, the sanctification of our relationships, of our whole lives. Every one of us can take part in that sanctification. We don't have to be farmers. Wherever two or three people are gathered in Christ's name, be they husband and wife, brothers or sisters, cousins or friends, there is Christ, blessing and being blessed, pouring out his grace and love upon us, filling us with the Holy Spirit, carrying on through us his work of saving and redeeming the world.

The Season of Christmas

Christmas
THE WORD

Readings
Midnight Isa 9:1-7; Tit 2:11-14; Lk 2:1-14
Dawn Isa 62:11-12; Tit 3:4-7; Lk 2:15-20
Day Isa 52:7-10; Heb 1:1-6; Jn 1:1-18

How well do you express yourself? If you are asked to make a speech, or to give your opinion, do you do yourself justice? There are people – and perhaps you are one of them – who are compassionate, and caring, and wise, and well-informed, but for some reason find it hard to express themselves in words, and come over as being dull or uncaring. On the other hand, there are people – many of them in the world of politics – who really are dull and uncaring, and callous, and cynical, and immoral, but who have the gift of the gab, and so come over as decent and sincere people.

Among human beings there is often a considerable difference between the inner personality, and the outward expression. We cannot suppose that this is so with God. It cannot be that God tells lies, or is economical with the truth, or is lost for words. Where God is concerned, the Word is, and must be, the perfect expression of the inner Being. The Word is the perfect image of God, indeed, the Word *is* God.

That Word has always existed, for as long as God has existed. There was never a time when God could not express himself, when he had to learn how to put his thoughts into words. Before the Big Bang, or whatever else was the first act of creation, God knew very well how to express himself. The whole creation, the galaxies and the stars, the sun and the moon and the earth, are all expressions of God's creative power. Do you want to hear the word of God? Look around you. If you can't hear the word of God in the sun and the moon and the stars, in the earth with its mountains and rivers and plants and animals, with its millions of men and women, so beautiful, so wise and so loving; if you can't hear the word of God in these his creatures, then you would not hear the word of God if he bellowed it in your ear through a megaphone.

This Word was made flesh and lived among us. We can look at this perfect image of God in Jesus and see what God is really like. And the contemplation of God's word in Jesus can correct many misconceptions about God. We might suppose, for example, that a God capable of creating the sun and the moon and the stars might be aloof, uncaring about the trivial affairs of mankind. But in Jesus we find that this is not so. The Word becomes flesh in the most humble of circumstances, becomes a little baby in a human family, concerned about the milk supply, and the provision of clean dry swaddling-clothes. As he grows up we find him concerned about the guests at a local wedding having enough wine to drink, about the health of his neighbours, about the plight of those who are excluded from society by their diseases or their occupations. Above all we find him concerned with justice, with those who are denied the means to live by the greed or indifference of those around them.

This is the inner reality of the God, as revealed by his perfect image. God is revealed as a God who cares. Nothing is too big for him to take care of, nothing is too small for his concern. Having seen the enormous power of God revealed in creation, we might take on trust his concern with great events like wars and earthquakes and the rise and fall of empires. But the tiny baby whose birth we celebrate reveals his concern with small things: small in comparison with great cataclysms, but still big enough to the likes of you and me: how we earn our living, how we get on with our wives or husbands, or with our children and parents; how we relate to one another; how we feel, what things have offended us, what things have angered us, what things have made us ashamed. All these things are of vital concern to God, who, his Word tells us, notices the death of a sparrow or the loss of a hair from our head.

Sunday in the Octave of Christmas
THE HOLY FAMILY

Readings
1 Sam 1:20-22.24-28; 1 Jn 3:1-2.21-24; Lk 2:41-52

On my wedding day, I noticed that my mother-in-law was crying. I said to her, 'Don't think of it as losing a daughter – think of it as gaining a son.' She said, 'That's why I'm crying.' We think it tragic when parents lose a child, but, one way or another, all parents lose their children. We lose our children through marriage, or when they grow up and leave home and move away. Even before that, they've begun to assert their independence, to make the point that they don't belong to us. We enjoy them for a while, but they're not ours to keep.

That point is brought home to Mary and Joseph when Jesus is twelve years old. They take him to Jerusalem for the feast. Afterwards they set out for home without him. That may seem very careless, but no doubt they were part of a large extended family. He would be with his grandparents, or his cousins or his aunts. Up to now that had been a perfectly safe assumption. But this time he wasn't with them. He had gone missing. Desperate with worry, they return to Jerusalem to look for him. They find him, eventually, in the Temple, and Mary says to him, 'Why have you done this to us? See how worried your father and I have been, looking for you.' And Jesus replies, 'Why were you looking for me? Did you not know I would be at my Father's?' The Greek phrase could mean, 'At my Father's house' or 'At my Father's business'. Probably Luke meant it to be ambiguous: Jesus is both in his Father's house, and about his Father's business. But the Father in question is not Joseph. It dawns, certainly on Mary, and perhaps on Joseph too, that Jesus has an agenda which is not theirs, business which is not theirs, things to teach which he has not learnt from them, loyalty to someone other than themselves.

We celebrate the feast of the Holy Family, but in fact our Gospel tells us of the beginning of the break-up of the Holy Family. This is the last time in the Bible that Joseph will be mentioned. We don't know what became of him. We assume that he died. Certainly from now on he is out of the picture. From now on, whenever there is mention of Jesus's father it is his heavenly Father who is meant. Jesus returns to Nazareth and spends another eighteen years there, but those years are hidden from us. The next time he is mentioned, he has left home. Only once afterwards does he return to Nazareth, and on this occasion the inhabitants try to throw him over a cliff. He is totally alienated from those friends and neighbours with whom he had used to travel to Jerusalem. The split which we see today developing between Jesus and his extended family has become a chasm.

I don't know whether any of this offers comfort to those whose children have moved away, not only physically, but mentally, emotionally, spiritually, from their parents, those whose children have adopted different ideas, different standards, perhaps even different religions, from those they learnt at home. It is hard to bear, but it has to be so. It was so for the Holy Family itself. Mary had to experience the pain that is common to so many parents.

The pain is necessary because Jesus needs the space to mature. He needs, as Saint Luke puts it, to increase in wisdom, in stature, and in favour with God and men. Had he remained part of one happy family, if he could always be assumed to be with the caravan of friends and relations, there would have been no Gospel, no crucifixion, no resurrection, no salvation. All this was part of God's plan.

It may be that the loss of our own children is also part of God's plan. I think of Saint Augustine's mother spending a whole night in prayer, praying that her son would not go away to Rome. He slipped away by night, even as she was praying; something of which he was afterwards ashamed, but if he had not gone, he would not have become a Christian, a bishop, a theologian, a saint. What wonderful things God has planned for our own children! Provided only that we have the wisdom to let them go, and the love to keep them in our prayers.

Second Sunday after Christmas
ENLIGHTEN THE EYES OF YOUR MIND

Readings
Ecclesus 24:1-2.8-12; Eph 1:3-6.15-18; Jn 1:1-18

Our Gospel has much to say about Christ the Light of the World: 'A light that shines in the dark, a light that darkness could not overpower.' He is 'the true light that enlightens all men.' Something of which even those in our country who are not religious have been reminded by the impressive number of lights which are lit to celebrate Christmas. I do not refer only to the candles which are lit at our Midnight Mass and carol services, but the lights which adorn the main streets of every town, the twinkling fairy-lights, the electric Father Christmasses which light up the front of so many houses. The proverbial man from Mars, arriving on earth at this time, would surely be able to grasp that we were celebrating the coming of light into our world.

What does this light do for us? Saint Paul tells us, 'May he enlighten the eyes of your mind so that you can see what hope his call holds for you, what rich glories he has promised the saints will inherit.' We do need the eyes of our mind enlightened, because there is so much in our world to darken them. We hear of children whose lives are darkened by abuse or neglect, of whole countries which are darkened by war, oppression, famine, and disasters of every kind. We ourselves may have experienced the darkness of sickness, depression, bereavement, guilt, stress or anxiety. Our world needs the light of Christ more than ever to illuminate its dark places.

Notice the liberality with which Christ sheds his light upon humanity. In his earthly life he encountered people who were blind, deaf, lame, despairing, suffering from every kind of assault from the forces of darkness. He did *not* say, 'Cheer up! Things may be bad for you now, but at the resurrection all will be made well.' Rather, he gave sight to the blind, hearing to the deaf, mobility to the lame, deliverance to those possessed by demons.

And this shows that he cares deeply about this life, here and now. Ours is not a religion which ignores the sufferings of this world because we hope that things will be better in heaven. Christ wants the fulness of life, health and happiness to his people here on earth, and he invites us to collaborate with him in bringing that fulness of life to all the people of the world. When we feed the hungry, minister to the sick, and bring comfort to those in distress, whether personally of through our support of dedicated charities, we are bringing Christ into the lives of those people.

Let us bring Christ into the life of someone today.

The Epiphany of the Lord
CAMELS

Readings Isa 60:1-6; Eph 3:2-3.5-6; Mt 2:1-12

Saint Jerome once remarked that ignorance of the scriptures is ignorance of Christ. That may seem like a blindingly obvious statement. Of course you will be ignorant of Christ if you haven't read the Gospel accounts of his life and teaching, or Saint Paul's estimate of his significance. But that is not what Saint Jerome meant. He was talking, not of the New Testament Scriptures, but of the Old Testament ones, and in particular of the prophets. Many features of the Christian tradition which the ignorant suppose are due to legend or pious imagination, are in fact perfectly scriptural, but the Scriptures are those of the Old Testament, not the New.

For example, every Christmas crib contains an ox and an ass. Saint Luke tells us that Mary laid Jesus in a manger, but he says nothing of an ox and an ass being present. Where do they come from? From Isaiah, chapter 1 verse 3, 'The ox knows its owner, and the ass its master's crib.' Or what about the three kings of orient, riding on their camels high and humpy? Saint Matthew says that the infant Jesus was visited by wise men, Magi, from the east; but he does not call them kings, nor does he mention their mode of transport. Where do we get the idea that they were kings?

From today's Psalm, number 71: 'The kings of Tarshish and the sea coasts shall pay him tribute. The kings of Sheba and Seba shall bring him gifts. Before him all kings shall fall prostrate, all nations shall serve him.' From very early times the Church has seen in the Magi the fulfilment of this prophecy, of kings coming from afar to worship the Christ. I once heard on the radio that 'later tradition suggested that one of the kings was black.' Nothing to do with later tradition: the Psalm tells us that 'The kings of Sheba and Seba shall bring him gifts.' Sheba is Ethiopia; the black one is the King of Sheba.

And what about the camels? They are from Isaiah, chapter 60: 'Camels in throngs will cover you, and dromedaries of Midian and Ephah; everyone in Sheba will come, bringing gold and incense.' Isaiah mentions the gold and incense which Matthew tells us were offered by the Magi. From the earliest times there has been agreement that the gold signifies that Christ is our king. Gold is a royal sort of gift. Kings need gold to make their coinage, or their crowns. Incense signifies that Christ is our God, for incense has been offered to God for many thousands of years. It was offered in the worship of the Temple, before the birth of Christ, and it is still used today.

The prophecy of Isaiah makes no mention of myrrh, the third gift of the Magi. Now myrrh is an aromatic spice used for embalming the dead. It signifies the sacrificial death Jesus was to die. Isaiah does not mention it because even he he did not understand that the Messiah had first to suffer before entering into his glory. Nobody did; they thought that the Messiah would immediately take possession of his kingdom and usher in a golden age. The disciples were stunned at the crucifixion, not only because of the horrific death which their leader had suffered, but because it seemed that God's own plan had failed and come to nothing.

And yet the suffering of the Christ was foretold in the prophets, indeed in the prophet Isaiah himself in his poems about the Suffering Servant; the risen Christ had to explain this to the disciples: 'You foolish men! So slow to believe the full message of the prophets! Was it not ordained that the Christ should suffer and so enter into his glory?' Then, starting with Moses and going through all the prophets, he explained to them the passages throughout the Scriptures that were about himself.

Some of the passages he would have pointed out were and are very familiar. For example, Isaiah chapter 53, 'And yet ours were the sufferings he bore, ours the sorrows he carried. But we, we thought of him as someone punished, struck by God, and brought low. Yet he was pierced through for our faults, crushed for our sins.' This seems as plain a prophecy as any of the sufferings of Christ. But the disciples had not made the connection, they had not understood that the Messiah, recognised by ox and ass and worshipped by wise men from the east, was the very same person who was to suffer and die for the expiation of their sins.

Let's not be hard on the disciples. It is very difficult to take in, all at once, the majesty of God's great plan. We absorb it little by little, week by week, feast by feast. Only when we have had the opportunity, over several years, to hear and ponder all the passages in the scriptures which are about Christ – his birth, his baptism, his teaching, his miracles, his suffering, his resurrection, his ascension, his sending of the Holy Spirit, his sitting at the right hand of the Father, his coming again in glory – only then do we appreciate the value of the great treasure we have been given, a good and perfect gift, a pearl of great price.

The Baptism of the Lord
THE STRAP OF HIS SANDALS

Readings
Isa 40:1-5.9-11; Tit 2:11-14; 3:4-7; Lk 3:15-16.21-22

What, we may ask, was so special about the strap of Jesus's sandals? Mark, Luke and John all have John the Baptist say that he wasn't worthy to undo the strap of Jesus's sandals. Matthew, curiously enough, has John say that he wasn't worthy to *carry* Jesus's sandals. But who would employ somebody to *carry* his sandals?

Imagine the scene, if you will. You are coming to John to be baptised. You must first take off your sandals. Perhaps you take off all your clothes, but certainly you take off your sandals – who goes paddling with his shoes on? It was a rather fiddly business, taking off your sandals. They would be tied with a leather strap, and perhaps one of John's disciples, or one of your own servants or friends, would help by undoing the straps. They might even stand on the bank holding your sandals as you were baptised – as Matthew puts it, *carrying* your sandals. These people would be performing a minor, but useful, part of the baptismal liturgy, rather like handing out the hymn books or bringing up the gifts at Mass.

So you see what John means. There is, he says, someone coming after him. John is not worthy to baptise him; indeed he is not worthy even to help him off with his sandals in preparation for baptism. Nevertheless, Jesus does submit to be baptised by John. It is almost a contest in humility, John declaring his unworthiness, Jesus nevertheless insisting on being baptised.

It's often pointed out that when *we* are baptised, the water makes us holy. Water has no power to make Jesus holy, but rather it is he who sanctifies the water. We could extend this principle to John. John cannot wash away the sins of Jesus – there are none to wash away. But by participating in this liturgy with him, Jesus washes away John's sins, shares a baptism with him, incorporates him into his kingdom.

It makes me think of the woman who washed the feet of Jesus with her tears, then anointed them with ointment. That incident is surely described in terms of a baptism. But it is not Jesus whose sins are washed away: he immediately says to the woman: '*Your* sins are forgiven.' I wonder if Jesus had *always* intended to wash his disciples' feet at the last supper, or whether it was this woman's action which suggested it to him. Did he think, 'What a beautiful thing! I must do this for my own disciples'?

Jesus tells us that whatever we do for the least of his brothers and sisters, we do for him. And whatever we do for him is immeasurably to our own advantage, calling down forgiveness, blessings and grace upon ourselves. What better way to celebrate the Baptism of Jesus than by baptising Jesus ourselves, by washing away his sins?

What an absurd thought! How can we, any more than John the Baptist, forgive the sins of the sinless Christ? But we *can* do so, when we forgive the sins of the least of his brothers and sisters. He has, after all, being gracious enough to accept all our sins as his own, and to bear their weight on the cross. And so, that person who annoyed us, that person who abused us or cheated us – we can forgive them. Let those offences be washed away and forgotten. Every time we forgive a wrong, freely, with all our heart, we baptise Christ, we wash his feet, we anoint him with the oil of gladness; and we bring down showers of blessings on our own heads.

Lent

First Sunday of Lent
EAT MY WORDS

Readings
Deut 26:4-10; Rom 10:8-13; Lk 4:1-13

The Devil said to Jesus, 'If you are the Son of God, tell this stone to turn into a loaf.' But Jesus replied, 'Scripture says: Man does not live on bread alone.' He was quoting freely from the Book of Deuteronomy. The exact quotation is, 'And he humbled you and let you hunger and fed you with manna ... that he might make you know that man does not live by bread alone, but that man lives by everything that proceeds out of the mouth of God.'

It is a curious idea, isn't it, that the Word of God should actually nourish us, like bread? The prophet Ezekiel was told, quite literally, to eat the Word of God: 'Son of Man, eat this scroll that I give you and fill your stomach with it.' Having digested this scroll, he is to go and proclaim God's message to the people of Israel. Like many curious stories in the Old Testament, this one is a sort of parable, and I think we can see the meaning clearly enough. Before Ezekiel can proclaim that message with credibility, he has first to digest it thoroughly himself. It's no good going to people and saying, 'It says here, in this book ... ' They won't take any notice of you unless you practise what you preach. In a sense, you have to *be* the book. So Ezekiel was made to digest the message, to make it part of himself, to *become* the message. Then he could go and proclaim it.

Every Catholic knows that at the Mass we eat the Body of Christ. And we ought also to know that Christ is the Word of God, the Word who, as St John says, was in the beginning with God, and was God, and was made flesh. But do we ever put two and two together and realise that at the Mass we are actually eating the Word of God, so that we can *become* the Word of God, and can therefore with credibility and conviction *proclaim* the Word of God?

Suppose Ezekiel had eaten the scroll, which, as he says, tasted like honey in his mouth; and then gone away and done nothing about it. Would God not have said, 'Ezekiel, you've missed the point. You're supposed to go away and proclaim the word you have eaten. Being made to eat that scroll was your commission to be a prophet.'

Eating the Word of God, whether we do so by listening to him in the Scriptures or by receiving him in the Holy Communion, is our commission to go out and proclaim the Word of God. Notice what a close connection Saint Paul makes between having the Word in our hearts and proclaiming it with our lips. 'Scripture says: the word, that is the faith we proclaim, is very near to you, it is on your lips and in your heart. If your lips confess that Jesus is Lord and if you believe in your heart that God raised him from the dead, then you will be saved. By believing from the heart you are made righteous; by confessing with your lips you are saved.' How odd it would be if we opened our hearts to receive the Word, then closed our lips when we should be proclaiming the wonderful works of God.

Second Sunday of Lent
TRANSFIGURATION

Readings
Gen 15:5-12.17-18; Phil 3:17–4:1; Lk 9:28-36

Peter, James and John see Jesus transfigured before their eyes; they see Moses and Elijah in glory, speaking of what Jesus is to accomplish in Jerusalem. They witness one of the most astonishing revelations of God's power breaking through into this world, that has ever been granted to anyone. Yet, only a few days later,

James and John will run away in terror at the arrest of Jesus, and Peter will deny three times that he even knows the man.

It may be that you and I, like Peter, James and John, have our darker moments, moments when our nerve fails, moments when we doubt whether what we believe is really true, whether Jesus really is the Son of God, whether he really is alive today, whether he can really do all things, whether indeed there is even a God who made the world and sent us his Son and raised him from the dead. It may be that the only way to avoid those darker moments is never to reflect on our faith at all, but simply to continue to believe what we were taught as children without stopping to think about it. I wouldn't recommend such an un-reflective faith, because it would be a shallow faith and it would fail us when really put to the test.

What I would recommend is that each of us treasure in our heart those moments when we were absolutely sure of our faith. It may be that each one of us has been given a moment when all was made clear, when we were vividly aware of the Father's love surrounding us and supporting us and enabling us to do things far beyond our natural abilities. If we can look back on those moments it may help us to keep the faith when we feel alone and vulnerable and afraid.

It may also help us through those dark moments if we are aware of a mistranslation in today's Mass. I am in a unique position to tell you this, because, as you may know, I am one of a team of scholars preparing the new translation of the Missal. The mistranslation to which I refer is in the preface of the Mass, where it says 'He wanted to teach them through the Law and the Prophets that the promised Christ had first to suffer and so come to the glory of his resurrection.' The Latin does not in fact refer solely to the sufferings of Christ. What it actually says is that it is necessary first to suffer in order to come to the glory of the resurrection. Necessary not only for Christ, but for you and me to suffer, before we come to the glory of our own resurrection. The sufferings we encounter in life are part of the deal. The illnesses, the disappointments, the bereavements, the scandals, the shame, the rejection, are part of the way of our own cross which must precede our own resurrection.

Third Sunday of Lent
BEARING FRUIT

Readings
Ex 3:1-8.13-15; 1 Cor 10:1-6.10-12; Lk 13:1-9

The people of Corinth were a bit too sure of themselves; or rather, they were a bit too sure of the Church. They had been baptised, they went to church, they received the Holy Sacrament; and that, they thought, was that. They were safe, however good or bad their personal behaviour might be.

Paul disabuses them of that mistake. He reminds them that the ancient Israelites had enjoyed a form of baptism in the Red Sea; they had enjoyed a form of communion, the bread of heaven which they called manna, and the miraculous drink that sprang from the rock. They had their equivalents of the sacraments of baptism and the Eucharist; but, as Saint Paul says, in spite of this, most of them failed to please God and their corpses littered the desert. The message is plain: it is not enough to belong to the Church and to receive the sacraments. We must bring forth the fruit of good works.

Jesus makes the same point in the Gospel. We should not delude ourselves with a false sense of security. It is not sufficient to be a limb of the true vine; we must bring forth good fruit; otherwise, we shall be lopped off. Jesus tells a parable: a fig tree is not bearing any fruit. The gardener suggests giving it one last chance; let him dig round it and manure it. If it still doesn't bear fruit, the owner can then cut it down.

If trees could think, I wonder what that tree would have thought as the gardener dug round its roots and poured in the manure. 'This is the life! What a wonderful tree I must be, that the gardener lavishes such care on me. None of these other trees is getting this treatment. I must be something very special.' Little did it know that all this was the prelude to getting the chop.

We also can delude ourselves. We have our churches, we have the inestimable privilege of hearing the word of God, and of receiving the Blessed Sacrament; we are given the enjoyment of singing God's praises, of experiencing fellowship and support from one another. The heavenly gardener is lavishing his care on us. But all these privileges are given to us for a purpose: that we should bear fruit for God.

How can we bear fruit for God? Surely we should make the firm resolution of doing some good deed, of doing some special kindness for someone, of telling someone the good news about Jesus Christ, of praying very earnestly for someone in trouble. If we have the intention, God will show us the opportunity.

The wonderful thing about our religion is, that whatever good thing we do, it counts towards the building up of God's kingdom and advances our salvation. Jesus tells us that whatever we did for the least of his brothers and sisters, we did for him. This makes life so much easier. We don't have to sit down and deliberate who is the most worthy recipient of our charity: we can come to the aid of anybody in need, and in that person we are coming to the aid of Christ. We don't need to wonder who is Christ's representative, so that we can pay him due honour. Everybody is Christ's representative. When we help the poor in the Third World, through *Trócaire* or CAFOD; when we visit a sick friend, when we give time to listen to a lonely or distressed person, whatever kindness we do, is done to Christ, and brings forth fruit for God.

Fourth Sunday of Lent
THE PRODIGAL SON

Readings
Josh 5:9-10; 2 Cor 5:17-21; Lk 15:1-3.11-32

The Fourth Sunday in Lent, in England and Ireland at any rate, is known as Mothering Sunday. We celebrate what is probably the hardest and most heartbreaking job ever invented, namely motherhood.

Of course, the Church never gets things quite right, and so our gospel story is all about fatherhood. We talk about the parable of the Prodigal Son, but actually the most interesting character in the story is the Father. Perhaps we should call it the Parable of the Forgiving Father, or the Indulgent Father, or the Loving Father. Again, the story is often cited as an example of repentance, but it's really about forgiveness.

The young man doesn't make much of a fist of repentance. He is the most repellent, self-centred character in the Bible. He can't wait for his father to die: he wants him as good as dead now, so that he can have his inheritance. Having got his hands on the money, he has no further interest in his father, and goes of to spend his patrimony in the grossest self-indulgence. Such people do not become saints overnight; nor does he. When the money runs out, he realises that he would be better off back with his father. His repentance, like everything he does, is motivated by self-interest.

And yet his father is willing to accept this half-hearted apology for repentance and welcome him back with all his heart. As the son comes into view, the father is standing at the door, looking for him in the distance. He sees his son a long way off, and goes running to meet him. He cuts short his son's carefully-rehearsed speech; he will hear nothing of taking him on as a hired servant. He kills the fatted calf and prepares a feast. There is nothing half-hearted about the father's joy at his son's return.

Our heavenly Father longs to have us come back to him, with a depth of desire which can only be hinted at by the desire of the father in the parable. God sent his Son to die in order to show us the intensity of that desire. His longing for our return far exceeds our feeble attempts at repentance.

And when we do come back to him, how we underestimate the Father's love! How little we appreciate the bonds of love which bind our heavenly Father to us! We come to him, shamefaced, not daring to look him in the eye, hoping at best to be taken on as hired servants. The psalmist suggests a quite different attitude: 'Look towards him and be radiant; let your faces not be abashed.'

The idea of having radiant faces when we look towards God comes from a story about Moses. We are told that when he went into the tabernacle to talk to God, his face would shine so brightly that he had to put a veil over it so as not to dazzle people. I wonder how radiant our faces are, as we leave church? I wonder what anyone passing by our church as we came out, would say about us? Would that person say, 'Those people's faces are radiant, shining with joy and happiness. It's as though they were coming from a meeting with God himself.' A face like that converts a lot of people. I think if I saw faces radiant with joy as they came out of a church, I should want to go into that church to see what was making those faces shine. Conversely, a guilty face like that of the Prodigal Son, or a sullen, angry face like that of his elder brother, will only turn people off. It might be worth our while having a mirror in our porch, with a notice saying, 'Please adjust your face before leaving.'

Fifth Sunday of Lent
TAKEN IN ADULTERY

Readings
Isa 43:16-21; Phil 3:8-14; Jn 8:1-11

The story of the woman taken in adultery was not part of Saint John's Gospel as originally written. The language and style are not those of Saint John. Our earliest and best manuscripts do not contain it. Those which do, insert it into different places in Saint John's Gospel. Some even insert it into Saint Luke's Gospel instead – where, actually, it fits in rather better. We are probably dealing with an early story about Jesus which was not part of any Gospel, but which people thought too important to be forgotten, and so inserted into places they thought suitable in the gospels.

We can easily see why they did not want it forgotten, for it shows Jesus refusing to condemn: 'Neither do I condemn you. Go away, and don't sin any more.' You may see why I said this story fits better into Saint Luke's Gospel, for Saint Luke's is pre-eminently the Gospel of non-condemnation. It is Saint Luke who records the parable of the Prodigal Son, that very unpleasant young man whose behaviour is totally unforgivable, but who is nonetheless forgiven. It is Saint Luke who tells how Jesus did not condemn Zacchaeus, the swindler, but asked for an invitation to dinner in his house. It is Saint Luke who records Jesus as saying, 'Father, forgive them, for they know not what they do.' Even on the cross, having suffered the worst that humanity has to offer, Jesus refuses to condemn.

How reluctant are *we* to condemn? I assume that we all have sufficient resources of Christian charity not to condemn the petty offences we encounter every day. Somebody has an outburst of anger: we don't condemn; no doubt that person is under some stress we know nothing about. Somebody steals a sum of money: we restrain our condemnation; perhaps that person was desperate. But how far up the scale *do* we go before we start to condemn? Adultery, assault, child abuse, murder? At what point on the scale does our charity break down?

In Jesus, we encounter the unconditional, infinite love of God, which goes all the way up the scale and still does not condemn. And that is very good news for us, because we can be sure that he does not condemn *us*. We bring our sins to him, our anger, our envy, our greed, so many things that make us ashamed, and we find, not condemnation, but acceptance, forgiveness and grace. 'Has no one condemned you? then neither do I condemn you. Go in peace, and sin no more.'

Passion (Palm) Sunday
THEOPHILUS

Readings
Procession Lk 19:29-40
Mass Isa 50:4-7; Phil 2:6-11; Lk 22:14–23:56

Once upon a time there was a man called Theophilus. He was an official, a civil servant in the Roman Empire. He became interested in a new religion which was becoming very popular in his area. It contained many things which sounded wonderful, stories of miraculous healings on earth and promises of everlasting life in heaven. But one aspect of it sounded very suspect. This new religion centred upon a man called Jesus, who had apparently been executed as a political agitator. Should a man like Theophilus, a member of the imperial service, have anything to do with a movement founded by a rebellious criminal?

Theophilus had a friend called Luke who was a prominent member of this new sect, and a personal friend of one of its leaders, a man named Paul. Theophilus asked Luke to give him an account of this new religion. Saint Luke responded by writing a book, which begins, in the rather elaborate and rhetorical style to which Theophilus was accustomed, 'Seeing that many others have undertaken to draw up accounts of the events that have taken place among us, exactly as these were handed down to us by those who from the outset were eyewitnesses and ministers of the word, I in my turn, after carefully going over the whole story from the beginning, have decided to write an ordered account for you, Theophilus, so that your Excellency may learn how well-founded the teaching is that you have received.'

Luke, in the Gospel which followed, was at pains to spell out one thing very clearly to Theophilus. This Jesus was not, as had been reported, a political agitator or a criminal. He was perfectly innocent, the victim of a miscarriage of justice. In his account of the trial and death of Jesus he has the Roman governor say, 'I have gone into the matter myself ... and found no case against him.' Again he has Pilate say, 'I have found no case against him that deserves death.' One of the criminals crucified with him had confessed, 'We are paying for what we did, but this man has done nothing wrong.' Even the centurion who crucified him had admitted, 'This was a great and good man.'

It is the *innocence* of Jesus which Luke stresses, rather than, say, his divinity, or the sacrificial nature of his death. And so the suffering and death of Jesus, according to Luke, is something he shares with all the innocent people of the world, who suffer for no fault of their own: all victims of miscarriages of justice; all who are imprisoned, or put to death, because of who they are rather than what they have done; victims of ethnic cleansing, murdered because they live in the wrong town; women and children done to death because they belong to the wrong tribe; innocent people shot or blown up because they belong to the wrong community. The suffering and death of Jesus is a powerful intercession for all such people, and a mighty sign of God's solidarity with them. All those locked up for crimes they did not commit can know that Jesus is there with them; he has been through all this. And less dramatically, those who suffer dark days of sickness, bereavement, loss of earnings, disappointment, failure – and that probably includes most of us – can know that Jesus is in the darkness with us.

Why should the innocent suffer? is a question that people have asked from the dawn of time; we find it on almost every page of the Bible. In his suffering and death, Jesus does not give us an answer to that question but shares in the suffering of all the innocent, transforms it by the power of his resurrection and carries it up to heaven, to the heart of God.

Paschal Triduum

Holy Thursday
YOU SHALL NEVER WASH MY FEET

Readings
Ex 12:1-8.11-14; 1 Cor 11:23-26; Jn 13:1-15

Peter would have done anything that Jesus commanded him. If Jesus had commanded him to wash the feet of the filthiest and most leprous beggar in Galilee, I'm sure Peter would have done it. What Peter found very hard was to let Jesus wash his own feet. His reluctance illustrates two points which we ourselves may find very difficult.

First, Peter is willing to do anything for Jesus, anything at all – except the one thing which Jesus does in fact want him to do. We too may be willing to offer our whole lives to Jesus – in fact we do so at every Mass, if we are attending properly to the meaning of it. We will go and evangelize China, if he bids us. But he doesn't bid us to do that; he bids us do something very ordinary, something which anybody could do, like washing up or hoovering the floor, or visiting a sick old woman - and that disappoints us. We feel we are capable of greater things, and that Jesus is underestimating us if he gives us such an ordinary task. Of course, that is our pride speaking, and Jesus gives us an example of humble service by performing the most menial task for his disciples. Washing feet does not require great intelligence, or great courage, or lengthy training. It merely requires humility, and that is the quality which Jesus would have us show.

Secondly, we may find it very hard to let someone else serve us. Peter would have washed the feet of a beggar, if Jesus commanded it, but he found it hard to submit to having his own feet washed. We may be willing to do a good turn for anyone, but find it very difficult to accept service from someone else. We like to be independent, we like to be in command, we do not like to admit our need. We prefer to wash our own feet. A small child allows its mother to wash its feet, and elderly people no longer able to look after themselves may submit to having their feet washed, but they do not like it. It is humiliating. Jesus asks us to submit to being humiliated.

The humiliation of having our feet washed is after all small compared with the humiliation Jesus was about to receive. On the following day he would be arrested and paraded before high priests and governors, jeered and mocked by soldiers, stripped naked and hung up on a cross for all to gawp at. As he prepared for this ordeal, Jesus did not want his disciples to show how brave and powerful they were. He wanted them to submit, in some small way, to share in his humiliation.

The washing of feet is not the most popular part of our Easter observance. Traditionally the priest washes the feet of twelve men, selected in advance. Not every parish *has* twelve men willing to undergo this ceremony; I'm not sure that this parish does. So we throw it open to anyone who is willing, male or female, young or old. I should be very happy to wash the feet of everyone here, if they would come forward. Consider what you would be willing to do for Jesus, all the many things you have promised from time to time to do for him. Well, the word is, he doesn't want you to do any of those things. He simply wants you to come forward and have your feet washed.

Good Friday
GOOD FRIDAY

Readings
Isa 52:13–53:12; Heb 4:14-16; 5:7-9; Jn 18:1–19:42

Today's service differs in several ways from any other service we perform, at any time during the Church's year. The beginning is

quite different: the priest enters in silence and prostrates himself
before the altar. At no other service does he do this. We see the
point, of course. What other response could he make to the
momentous event which we celebrate, than to throw himself on
the ground, without a word? Or, if a word comes into his mind,
it must be, 'Lord, have mercy.'

Then, we have the long reading of the Passion according to
Saint John. This is not entirely unique: on Palm Sunday we also
have a reading of the Passion, from one of the other gospels.
But it is one of only two occasions in the year, when we read, in
its entirety, the story of Christ's saving sacrifice.

There follow the prayers. Two things distinguish them from
those offered on any other day. One is their form: an invitation
to pray, followed by a period of silent prayer, followed by a collect
sung by the priest. This is not how we pray on other days. And
the second distintuishing mark of these prayers is their scope. We
pray for everyone, for the Pope, the Bishops, all God's people,
believers and unbelievers, the Jewish people, those in any kind
of trouble or distress. Nobody is left out, because Christ's blood
was poured out for all people. It was poured out for those who
believed in him and those who crucified him, for those who
abandoned him and those who betrayed him. We dare not refuse
to pray for any soul for whom Christ died.

Next comes the unveiling and veneration of the cross. This
is a strange practice. Naturally we would wish to venerate our
Saviour, but we do not venerate him directly; rather, we venerate the wood of the cross on which he died. Why should we pay
honour to an instrument of torture and execution? Because it is
the instrument of our salvation. The tree of shame and death has
become the tree of life for us. It is the supreme example of how
God can bring good out of evil: he takes something fashioned
to cause pain and makes of it the means of eternal happiness.

Finally, we receive Communion. We do not celebrate Mass
today. From the earliest times Christians have shrunk from offering the sacrifice on the very day when Christ offered his one
all-sufficient sacrifice of himself; instead we receive hosts reserved

from the celebration of the Lord's Supper last night. Though we do not celebrate the Mass, in the act of Communion we join ourselves to the body broken for us on the cross.

Why are there so many unique, or at least unusual, features in today's Liturgy? Because the event we celebrate is utterly unique, quite unlike any other throughout history. On what other day has the Son of God ever offered himself in sacrifice, and died for us? On what other day has he borne our sufferings, or carried our sorrows, as he has today? What other sacrifice, before or since, has been so efficacious? What other day commemorates so much grace poured out for us? On what other day has our supreme high priest gone through to the highest heaven? On what other day should we be so confident in approaching the throne of grace, or more certain that we shall shall find mercy from God, and grace when we are in need of help?

The Easter Season

Easter Vigil
PASSING THROUGH THE SEA

Readings
Gen 1:1–2:2; Gen 22:1-18; Ex 14:15–15:1;
Isa 54:5-14; Isa 55:1-11; Bar 3:9-15.32–4:4; Ezek 36:16-28
Rom 6:3-11; Mt 28:1-10

The passage through the Red Sea has always been seen as a symbol, both of Christian baptism and of Christ's death and resurrection.

The connexion with baptism is the more obvious: the Israelites pass through a body of water, leaving behind their old life as slaves in Egypt and entering into a new life in the promised land. Their oppressors, the Egyptians, are drowned. In the same way Christians, passing through the waters of baptism, have their sins washed away and drowned, they leave behind their old lives and enter the promised land of God's kingdom. There are many customs associated with baptism which bring out the meaning of the rite: for example, clothing the candidate in a new white garment, signifying the new life they are taking on. One custom which, perhaps unfortunately, has not survived from the early Church is to give the candidates a meal of milk and honey, signifying that they have entered, to use the biblical phrase, a land flowing with milk and honey.

The connexion between the Red Sea and Christ's death and resurrection is perhaps not so obvious, but it is already alluded to in the New Testament. At the Transfiguration, Moses and Elijah talk with Jesus about the Exodus which is about to accomplish in Jerusalem; and the term 'Exodus' is surely carefully chosen. The passage through the Red Sea was God's great act of deliverance for the people of Israel; Christ's death and resurrection is God's great act of deliverance for all people, delivery from slavery to sin and to self.

All these ideas are linked together by Saint Paul in his Letter to the Romans.

> When we were baptised in Christ Jesus we were baptised in his death; in other words, when we were baptised we went into the tomb with him and joined him in death, so that as Christ was raised from the dead by the Father's glory, we too might live a new life.

Baptism is not very obviously like death, if we think only of death by crucifixion; but if we think of death by drowning, then the connexion is clearer. And in the early Church, baptism was much more like drowning, as the candidates were plunged into a pool of water, or into a river. Merely to pour a little water over their head is not such a clear sign of drowning; and yet it *is* true baptism; Christ's power to save does not depend upon the quantity of water we use when we baptise. Those we baptise with a little water on the head, share in the death and resurrection of Jesus, as surely as if we plunged them to the very bottom of the sea – which, I dare say, is a great relief for them.

Being baptised, they enter upon the new life, the life of grace in Jesus Christ, being fed, if not on milk and honey, then with something far greater, the body and blood of Christ himself. This life of grace they share with us and with all Christians. Christ, our good shepherd, having laid down his life for his sheep and risen from the dead, leads us beside the still waters of baptism, anoints our head with the oil of chrism and prepares a banquet before us, the banquet of his own body and blood, the banquet of which Saint Paul writes, 'Christ our passover has been sacrificed for us; come, let us celebrate the feast.'

Easter Sunday
RUNNING

Readings
Acts 10:34.37-43; Col 3:1-4; (1 Cor 5:7-8); Jn 20:1-9

Everything in Saint John's account of the Resurrection speaks of urgency. Mary of Magdala comes very early to the tomb, while it is still dark. She cannot wait until the sun is up. When she finds the tomb empty she does not walk, but runs, to Simon Peter. Peter and the other disciple do not walk to the tomb, they run. The other disciple, perhaps younger and fitter than Peter, runs faster. Everyone is running, everyone is in haste. Something very important has happened.

If we were at the Holy Sepulchre today, we would see something of that urgency, for we should see someone emerge from the tomb carrying the Easter flame, the Light of Christ, and he would not walk, but run the length of the church, like an Olympic sprinter. He would not be singing about the resurrection, but rather shouting about it at the top of his voice. People would be fighting each other to get a light from his torch. There would be real danger of broken limbs in the mêlée. There would be little decorum, little restraint, about the proclamation. It might not be suit our western sense of propriety. It might not seem like a religious service at all. Perhaps it might seem more like the scenes of jubilation in the streets of London at the end of the second world war. And yet, which was more significant, our war with Hitler, or God's war with Satan?

How sedately, in comparison, do we in the west announce the resurrection of our God. The priest slowly and solemnly raises the paschal candle, and intones, 'Christ our Light!' He walks gravely up the aisle and sings the proclamation a second and a third time. His manner speaks, no doubt, of something of some importance. But does it speak of God's victory in the war with evil, of the end of death, of absolute and eternal life bursting into the shadows of our world?

No doubt, we are rather restrained in the way we do our liturgy; but are we just as restrained in the way we pass on the stupendous message of the Resurrection? What did the disciples do after they found that Jesus had risen from the dead? Why, they told everybody about it. They told the other disciples, they told their friends, they went out into the street and told everybody they met. This was news indeed, the greatest news ever.

When we have finished celebrating the Resurrection, will we tell anyone else about it? Or will we go home, turn on the television, and forget about it for another year?

Second Sunday of Easter
THE WOUNDS OF CHRIST

Readings
Acts 5:13-16; Rev 1:9-13.17-19; Jn 20:19-31

Thomas was not present with the disciples when the risen Jesus appeared to them. They told him that the Lord was risen, but he would not believe.

Why did he not believe? Did he suppose that his dearest friends would invent such a story, to deceive him? Did he suppose that they had been mistaken on such a vitally important matter? Did he suppose that they had seen a ghost? We don't know.

But we do know what finally convinced him. It was the wounds of Christ. Jesus invited him to put his fingers into the holes in his hands, and to put his hand into his wounded side. That was enough for Thomas. 'My Lord and my God!' he exclaimed, and he believed. The wounds vouched for the reality of the apparition; a ghost does not have wounds in his hands and his side.

I sometimes wonder whether those wounds still hurt, after the resurrection. When the risen Jesus had said to Mary Magdalen, 'Do not touch me, for I have not yet ascended to the Father' – was her touch actually painful? Perhaps that suggestion is ludicrous, but certainly the burning love for our race that had brought Jesus to the cross still persisted, and persists for ever. Perhaps the pain which that love had imposed still persisted too.

Many Christians have a great devotion to the five wounds of Christ. They are often represented in art. Traditionally, a church building, which is an image in stone of the Body of Christ, is pierced by five doors, representing his five wounds. Walk around a medieval church, and you will often find that this is so. There may be two at the west end, leading out through a north and south porch, one at the the east end leading out to the sacristy, another to the bell tower, and often you will find a little door in the side of the church, perhaps never opened, and put there for no other reason than to make up the number five.

Saint Francis, and some other saints, have had such a devotion to the wounds of Christ that they have themselves received the stigmata, wounds in their own bodies matching those of Christ. Whether or not the risen Christ felt pain in his wounds, those who have received the stigmata seem to feel real pain, and the share they receive in the sufferings of Christ is the very point of the miracle.

We may not have received the stigmata, but probably all of us – certainly all of us who have reached the age of maturity – will have received wounds of one sort or another. Perhaps real physical wounds, from accident or illness; the wounds of grief, of sadness, of guilt, of disappointment, of despair, of anger, of inner turmoil, of self-doubt, of shame, of betrayal. That's a lot more than five wounds, but so many experiences in life inflict so many wounds.

These wounds are probably not very pretty, and I dare say we try to keep them covered up. It may be very painful to expose them to be gazed upon and touched by others.

And there is a real risk in exposing our wounds. There are people who prey on the wounded, as a lion might prey on a wounded deer. But if we can bring ourselves to reveal our wounds, it is remarkable how much more real we become. Real people have wounds; and if we say that we have no wounds, people will not believe in us. If we are allowed to see someone else's wounds, we think, Yes, that person is real, that person is like me, I've suffered like that, I can relate to that pain.

I think too that we commend our religion most effectively when we do not hide our own wounds. There are people who try to propagate their faith by looking quite obscenely happy, who go around saying that they have had no worries, no cares, no trials or tribulations, since they gave themselves to Jesus. I don't know if they ever convert anybody. I myself could never take seriously anyone who claimed to be a follower of Christ, and yet had no wounds to show for it.

Third Sunday of Easter
PETER

Readings
Acts 5:27-32.40-41; Rev 5:11-14; Jn 21:1-19

You can go today to the spot beside the Sea of Galilee where the risen Jesus took breakfast with his disciples. They've built a chapel on the spot, sticking out into the sea. Some years ago they cut an extra door into that chapel, so that Pope Paul VI, arriving by boat, could step straight out of the boat into the church. Pope Paul wanted to arrive by boat to show that he, like Saint Peter before him, was a fisherman.

There's a good deal in the Gospel reading about fishing, and about being fishers of men. That wonderful catch of fish, 153 of them, represents the great harvest of souls we are called upon to catch. I'll spare you the mathematics, but the number 153 signifies completeness, the entire world, all the peoples in the world. And there is room for all the people of the world in the Church, which is represented by the net. It will not tear, though at times it will stretch and feel the strain of such great diversity.

What moved me most about that spot beside the Sea of Galilee, is a sculpture which has been erected there. It shows Peter kneeling, and Jesus stretching out one hand over him in a gesture of reconciliation, and with the other hand giving him his pastoral staff. It illustrates the dialogue that Jesus has with Peter in the Gospel story. Three times Jesus asks Peter to affirm that he loves him; thus atoning for the three times Peter had denied him. Three times Jesus asks Peter to feed his sheep.

This shows us, if we need to be shown, that a pastor is not chosen because he is better than other people. He is just as much in need of forgiveness and reconciliation as anyone else, perhaps more so. The grace which reconciles is the same grace which strengthens and ordains. If any one has sinned grievously, has behaved abominably and unforgivably: then perhaps that person should seriously consider a vocation to the priesthood.

We should all, whether saints or sinners, consider very carefully the last sentence of the Gospel reading: 'When Jesus had finished speaking he said to him, Follow me.' When Jesus had finished speaking, that is, when he had finished proclaiming the Gospel, when he had finished teaching by word and example, he invited Peter to respond by following him.

He offers us that same invitation: 'Follow me.' We may be apprehensive about following Jesus; after all, the Scriptures give us a glimpse of where that road may lead: through weary deserts, over stormy seas, perhaps to the cross. But if that thought fills us with trepidation, we should raise our eyes to see where that road ends, where Christ now sits in majesty at the right hand of the Father, worshipped by the saints and the holy angels. That is the destination to which he is calling us when he says, 'Follow me.'

Fourth Sunday of Easter
THE GOOD SHEPHERD

Readings
Acts 13:14.43-52; Rev 7:9.14-17; Jn 10:27-30

If you read through Saint John's Gospel, one of the first things you notice is that Jesus is presented in a very different way from that of the other three Gospels. In the other three Gospels, the Synoptic Gospels as we call them, Jesus teaches by means of parables: he will tell the parable of the Good Samaritan, or of the Prodigal Son. There are no parables in Saint John's Gospel; what we find instead are a number of great 'I am' statements which Jesus makes about himself: I am the Bread of Life; I am the Light of the World; I am the Resurrection; I am the Way, the Truth and the Life; and so on.

We find in the Synoptic Gospels a parable about a good shepherd. If he has a hundred sheep and one of them goes missing, he leaves the other ninety-nine in the wilderness and goes in search of the lost one; and when he finds it, he brings it home on his shoulders.

We do *not* find that parable in Saint John's Gospel; instead, we find Jesus saying:

I am the good shepherd. The good shepherd is one who lays down his life for his sheep. The hired man, since he is not the shepherd and the sheep do not belong to him, abandons the sheep and runs away as soon as he sees a wolf coming. I am the good shepherd, and I lay down my life for my sheep.

The teaching is the same as that in the parable, but it is made more explicit. It is made clear that the Good Shepherd loves his sheep not only to the extent of incurring hardship and danger for them – we could infer that from the parable – but to the extent of actually laying down his life for them.

I said that the teaching is the same as in the parable, but in fact there is a difference of emphasis. In the parable, Jesus's concern is not with the ninety-nine sheep; they are left to fend for themselves in the wilderness. Jesus goes after the prodigal, the lost sheep, the stray, as we see him going after Zacchaeus or Matthew. Saint John makes it clear that Jesus nevertheless cares for the whole flock. It shows him tending the flock:

> The sheep that belong to me listen to my voice; I know them and they follow me. I give them eternal life; they will never be lost and no one will ever steal them from me.

How often do we ponder the fact, that we belong to a very special flock which is watched over by the Good Shepherd? Do we more often feel like a lonely sheep, a sheep that is not part of a flock, a lost sheep, a sheep without a shepherd? And yet the most important thing our religion tells us is that we *are* loved, we *are* cared for. God loved the world so much, that he sent his Son to be the Good Shepherd who would lay down his life for us. We are his flock; you and I individually are sheep of that flock; and even if we should wander far away from it, the Good Shepherd still cares passionately about us, and puts himself out to fetch us back from the wilderness in which we get ourselves lost, and brings us back to the flock.

Fifth Sunday of Easter
DOORS

Readings
Acts 14:21-27; Rev 21:1-5; Jn 13:31-35

On returning to Antioch, Paul and Barnabas gave an account of what God had done with them, and how he had opened the door of faith to the pagans.

Often, during Eastertide, our readings speak to us of opening doors, of opening locks. We hear of the risen Jesus appearing in the upper room, though the doors were locked. The disciples had locked the doors to keep their enemies out; but they were also keeping the Gospel locked in, and Jesus does not care to have his Gospel locked in. So he appeared to them and said, 'As the Father sent me, so am I sending you' – in other words, 'Open those doors, get out there and proclaim my Gospel.'

We read of the apostles, a few days later, being arrested and locked up in the common gaol. But at night the angel of the Lord opened the prison gates and said as he led them out, 'Go and stand in the Temple, and tell the people all about this new life.' In other words, 'Get out through those gates and proclaim the Gospel.'

In yet another Easter reading we hear Jesus say, 'I am the gate of the sheepfold ... I am the gate. Anyone who enters through me will be safe: he will go freely in and out.' Jesus is himself the gate, and he doesn't take kindly to anyone else setting himself up as the gate or door, to stop people coming in to him, or to stop the Gospel coming out to them.

And so this week, we hear of this great missionary journey of Paul and Barnabas: through Lystra and Iconium to Antioch in Pisidia, through Pisidia to Pamphylia, Attalia and finally by ship back to Antioch in Syria. Just names to us, names of faraway places, some of them no longer on the map; but actually the record of an enormously important missionary journey, covering many hundreds of miles, the first time that the Church had ever attempted such a thing. It is because of that journey, and other even more ambitious journeys which Paul undertook, that we are Christians today. Rightly did they describe this wonderful undertaking as opening the door of faith to the pagans.

Jesus is the door; but with him and in him we are also doors. Do we keep our door open, or closed? Do people come in, through us, and find Jesus? Or do we lock them out? Does the Gospel go out from us to our friends, our families, our neighbours? Or do we keep it locked in?

Now I take it that whatever the answer to that question is, all of us would *want* to be an open door for Jesus. And so let's try to be a door through which at least one person can come in and find Jesus.

Perhaps if we keep that door open we may find that the person who comes in is Jesus himself, to make his home within our heart, and fill us with joy and love.

And let's try to be a door through which the Gospel can go out – I don't say to Lystra and Iconium, but to one person: surely there is one person with whom we can share the good news? Actually let's not forget about Lystra and Iconium, and all the other distant parts of the world. We may not be able to go to the ends of the world ourselves, but we can support the Church's mission to every corner of the globe. Only Paul and Barnabas, just two men, went to Lystra and Iconium and Pisidia and Pamphylia; but they had a pretty impressive support group at home who were praying for them, encouraging them, providing the necessary financial support, perhaps writing to people they knew in those regions, preparing the way for Paul and Barnabas, opening doors for them.

None of us need ever say we have no opportunity to spread the Gospel. If we have the right intention, if we make this the subject of our prayers, Jesus will show us a door. Then it only remains for us to open it.

Sixth Sunday of Easter
HOME

Readings
Acts 15:1-2.22-29; Rev 21:10-14.22-23; Jn 14:23-29

There are many Marian shrines in the world: Lourdes and Fatima, Knock and Medjugorje, and many others. My own personal favourite is Walsingham, in Norfolk.

I wonder if you know what happened there? In the year 1061 the Blessed Virgin appeared there to a lady called Richeldis. She asked Richeldis to build a house for her in Walsingham. This would be a replica of the Holy House in Nazareth where the Holy Family had lived. Not everyone had the means to travel to Nazareth, so Walsingham would be 'England's Nazareth' and a pilgrimage to Walsingham would be just as good as a visit to the real Nazareth.

For me the special thing about Walsingham is that our Lady asked Richeldis to build her a home here in England. When we visit Walsingham we are calling on our Lady, and all the Holy Family, in their home. We are not unwelcome guests: Mary's whole purpose was to issue an invitation to all the people of England to visit her there.

Now a home is a different thing from a church or a palace. We may put on our Sunday best to come to church or to visit a palace. But the essential thing about a home is that it is homely. We come as we are, we take off our shoes, we make ourselves at home. And it is a wonderful privilege that Mary has offered to be at home to all who care to call on her in Walsingham.

There is too, in the Gospel, a beautifully homely touch. Jesus says to his disciples, 'If anyone loves me he will keep my word, and my Father will love him, and we shall come to him and make our home with him.' You don't have to come to us, no, *we* shall come to *you* and make our home with *you*. We build magnificent cathedrals for God, but he says, Never mind those: I shall come and make my home with anyone who loves me. What sort of homes do we have, that God the Father, Creator of the universe, with his Son Jesus Christ and the Holy Spirit, the Advocate, should want to come and live in them?

Home is where your heart is, says the proverb; and God literally wants to make his home where our heart is, in our heart itself. A popular hymn has the line, 'In your hearts enthrone him'. No doubt, he does really want to set up his throne in our heart. But perhaps 'throne' is too grand a term. A throne is a splendid thing, all covered with gold. But I've never yet seen a throne that looked very comfortable. Jesus doesn't say, 'We shall make our palace in him.' He says, 'We shall make our *home* in him.'

Perhaps we should offer God, not a throne, but an armchair, a comfortable chair. He wants to be comfortable with us, at ease with us; and he wants us to be comfortable with him.

How comfortable *are* we with God? How comfortable are we with the thought of coming face to face with him? Do we dread the judgement to come? Or do we long to come face to face with our loving Father, the Father who loved us so much that he sent his Son to die for us?

'Peace I bequeathe to you,' says Jesus, 'My own peace I give to you.' Do we enjoy that peace, or do we feel restless, disturbed, ill at ease, as we consider the course of our life?

'Do not let your hearts be troubled or afraid.' *Are* our hearts troubled or afraid as we look forward to the end of this life and our eternal destiny in the next? Or do we think of it as coming home to the God who came so kindly, to make his home with us?

The Ascension of the Lord
ASCENSION

Readings
Acts 1:1-11; Heb 9:24-28; 10:19-23; Lk 24:46-53

What is the importance of the feast of the Ascension? What do we learn from it? What would we have missed if we hadn't come?

In a way, the Ascension is the most important feast of all, for it is the culmination and the conclusion of Christ's ministry on earth. After his resurrection, he did not hang about in this world to die all over again. As Saint Paul says, Christ, having been raised from the dead, will never die again. Death has no power over him any more. He appeared on earth to demonstrate the truth of the resurrection; as Saint Luke says, 'He had shown himself alive to them after his Passion by many demonstrations: for forty days he had continued to appear to them and tell them about the kingdom of God.' But these appearances would not go on for ever. His mission on earth complete, he took his throne in heaven and began his reign.

In doing so he fulfilled many prophecies of the Scriptures, for example that found in the Book of Daniel:

> On him was conferred sovereignty, glory and kingship, and men of all peoples, nations and languages became his servants. His sovereignty is an eternal sovereignty which shall never pass away, nor will his empire ever be destroyed.

Today is the true feast of Christ the King; I am not sure why we need another one in the autumn.

A second thing to understand about the Ascension is that when Christ ascended into heaven, he took up with him something which he did not bring down with him: our human nature. Humanity, our nature, is taken up to heaven and is seated with him, and in him, at the right hand of the Father. In the words of the hymn appointed for Evening Prayer today,

> The Lord goes up with shouts of joy,
> With trumpets all his triumph tell;
> With him humanity is raised
> Above angelic worlds to dwell.

It is Christ's Ascension that makes heaven our true home, and gives us the hope of ascending there ourselves, so that where he is, we may be also.

A third thing to understand about the Ascension is that Christ, having been raised from the dead and exalted into heaven, is seated at the right hand of the Father and there he intercedes for us. Constantly he is pleading for us. This is why we conclude so many of our prayers with the formula, 'Through Christ our Lord.' Our own prayers might seem to count for little, but we know that Christ takes them up and offers them to the Father on our behalf; and his prayer is most certainly heard.

There was once a bishop who made a visit to a Church school. He asked the children some questions. First, he asked, 'Who can tell me where Jesus was born?' At once, a hand went up, and attached to the hand was a smart little girl in the front row. 'Please sir,' she said, 'Jesus was born in Bethlehem.' Then the bishop said, 'And who can tell me where Jesus was crucified?' Another hand went up, this one attached to a smart little boy, also in the front row. 'Please sir,' he said, 'Jesus was crucified in Jerusalem.' Then the bishop asked, 'And who can tell me: Where is Jesus *now*?' There was a silence. The smart little girl didn't know. Nor did the smart little boy. But then a hand went up in the back row, a rather dirty little hand attached to a scruffy little boy. It was not a hand that went up very often. The teacher's heart sank, for this little boy was not known for delivering many correct answers. But the teacher need not have worried. The little boy said, 'Please sir, he's in heaven, asking God to give us another chance.'

Seventh Sunday of Easter
INTERCESSION

Readings
Acts 7:55-60; Rev 22:12-14.16-17.20; Jn 17:20-26

In the Church we use a number of big words whose meaning is not always obvious. A case in point is the word 'intercession'. We commonly talk of intercession as though it meant simply 'prayer'. Somebody gets up and says the prayers at Mass, and we all think those are the intercessions. Actually intercession means 'stepping in'. It means stepping in between two people having a fight – which is a quick way of getting two black eyes. An intercessor is a middle-man, a go-between.

Jesus is our intercessor, the middle-man between God and humanity. He is able to be so because he is both God and man. And so he speaks to us on God's behalf, and speaks to God on our behalf. We see him doing both these things in John's Gospel. First, he speaks to his disciples about God, and tells them things they had never dreamt of, about the Holy Spirit, the Advocate, whom the Father will send in his name.

Having spoken to the disciples about God, he now turns and speaks to God about the disciples. He doesn't have to *tell* his Father about the disciples; the Father knows already. What he does instead is to pray for his disciples.

And having prayed for his immediate disciples, those who were seated at the table with him, he goes on, as we read in the Gospel, 'I pray not only for these, but for those also who through their words will believe in me.' That is, for you and me, and for all his Church. It is a wonderful prayer, if you care to read it through. He prays, 'Father, I want those you have given me – that again is you and me – to be with me where I am, so that they may always see the glory you have given me.' And what he prays most earnestly, over and over again, is 'May they all be one. Father, may they be one in us, as you are in me and I am in you.'

Well, if we are to be one in Jesus, we must be the same as he is. Just as he is our intercessor, so we must be intercessors. And that doesn't just mean people who say prayers. It means go-betweens, middle-men and middle-women. We are to be the links between God and all mankind. All of us, not just missionaries, are called to proclaim the Good News. That indeed is the purpose of Jesus's prayer for us. For he says, 'Father, may they be one in us, as you are in me and I am in you, so that the world may believe it was you who sent me.' We are to be the instruments through which all the world may believe in God, and in the Son whom he has sent.

What are we doing to be intercessors, middle-men and middle-women between God and the world? Or if that seems too tall an order, what are we doing to be the intercessor between God and the family next door, between God and our best friend, between God and the people we work with, between God and our children, our godchildren, our grandchildren?

Some people are doing quite a lot. I think of children who make their first Communion. Their parents, who have communicated the faith to them, have every right to think of themselves as intercessors on behalf of their children. And, no doubt, there are godparents, grandparents, catechists and teachers who could with justice call themselves intercessors for those children.

I think of some friends of mine who have been received into the Church; I would like to think of myself as an intercessor on their behalf.

If you step in between two people fighting you get two black eyes. Jesus himself suffered to be our intercessor: he felt the full weight of the hatred that had sprung up between mankind and God. If we are truly intercessors, it will hurt. It's wonderful to see our children remaining steadfast in the faith; it can be very painful to see them fall away. I shared my own faith with a couple of friends, and I take pleasure in seeing them make that faith their own. More often, I have had the pain of seeing friends reject or ignore that faith. But the pain is small compared with the glory that is promised us, the glory that the Father gave to Jesus, and which he shares with us, and which we shall enjoy to the full with our children and friends before the throne of grace and glory.

Pentecost Sunday
PENTECOST

Readings
Acts 2:1-11; Rom 8:8-17; Jn 14:15-16.23-26

We give one another gifts at Christmas. Perhaps it would be just as appropriate to give one another gifts at Pentecost, because it is the feast when we celebrate God giving to us the gifts of the Holy Spirit. Consider the story of the outpouring of the Holy Spirit. The disciples are gathered together in one room, when they hear the sound as of a powerful wind from heaven, and they see tongues of flame descending on the heads of each of them. Filled with the Holy Spirit, they rush out and proclaim the Good News in many different tongues, so that all the many nations represented in Jerusalem hear them preaching in their own language about the marvels of God.

What gifts did the apostles receive? Most obviously, the gift of tongues. That was certainly the most spectacular of the gifts they received.

But no less remarkable was the spirit of courage. Before the outpouring of the Holy Spirit they had been timorous, hiding behind locked doors in the upper room, for fear of their enemies. But now they instantly rushed out of those doors, and proclaimed the Good News with all boldness.

And again, they received the spirit of understanding. Often the Gospel tells us that the disciples did not understand something Jesus had told them, because they had not yet received the Holy Spirit. Jesus acknowledged the limits to their understanding when he said, 'I still have many things to say to you, but they would be too much for you now. But when the Spirit of truth comes he will lead you to the complete truth.' And when the Holy Spirit does come, he does indeed give them understanding, sufficient understanding to go out and proclaim things which had mystified them before.

In the sacrament of Confirmation we experience our own personal Pentecost. We receive the sevenfold gifts of the Spirit: the spirit of wisdom and understanding, the spirit of right judgement and courage, the spirit of knowledge and reverence, the spirit of wonder and awe. I have sometimes discussed with our confirmation candidates which of those gifts they need the most. I think most of them feel that they need the spirit of courage, because there are many things in the world which intimidate you if you are trying to live the Christian life.

Which gift do *you* need the most? Remember that the traditional seven are not the only ones on offer. Saint Paul tells us about other gifts of the Holy Spirit: love, joy, peace, patience, kindness, goodness, trustfulness, gentleness and self-control. Which of them would be of most benefit to *you*? Perhaps there are things in your life which irritate and upset you. No doubt, you would benefit from the gift of patience. Sometimes life can seem very joyless, an endless grind of work, responsibility, stress, lack of reward. If you feel like that, then surely you need the gift of joy. Perhaps you are troubled, you can't sleep; things you have done, or left undone, keep forcing themselves into your mind. You need the gift of peace. Perhaps you are always on edge, you have a tendency to fly off the handle. Perhaps you need the gifts of gentleness and self-control.

I'm going to cut my homily short now and sit down. I've told you the theory, but I want you, for a couple of minutes, to do the practical. For a few moments, I want you to ask yourself, 'What is missing in *my* life? What do I need from the Holy Spirit to put it right?' And then you can quietly pray, 'Come, Holy Spirit, and give me the gift of … '

I'll let you finish the sentence yourself.

Solemnities of the Lord

Trinity Sunday
TRINITY

Readings
Prov 8:22-31; Rom 5:1-5; Jn 16:12-15

One of my favourite television comedy shows was called 'Allo, Allo.' And one of the funniest moments in that show was when the girl from the Résistance said, 'Listen very carefully: I shall say this only once.'

You can't say that in the Church. If you said something only once, people wouldn't take it in. Jesus acknowledges that in the Gospel: 'I still have many things to say to you, but they would be too much for you now.' How often has a priest cut a homily short because, although he still had many useful and true and edifying things to say, he knew that his congregation could take in only so much. Often we have to tell ourselves that there will be other homilies, there will be other discussions, there will be other books and articles, to lead people further along the road: we don't have to tell the whole story now. Which is just as well, or else homilies would stretch on for hours.

Jesus, in his talk to the disciples at the Last Supper, begins to reveal to them the mysteries of the Holy Trinity. He who has seen Jesus has seen the Father: the Father is in the Son and the Son in the Father. The disciples will receive the Holy Spirit, sent by the Father in response to the prayer of the Son. These were mysteries indeed, and the disciples must have been astonished. But eventually Jesus saw that their eyes were glazing over: they could take in no more. So he assured them that when the Spirit of Truth came he would lead them to the complete truth. The revelation of the Trinity was not to be a case of 'Listen very carefully: I shall say this only once.' Rather, it was a process, a road on which the disciples would gradually advance, led by the Spirit, deeper and deeper into the mystery.

Saint Paul hints at a similar process when he says that our sufferings bring patience, and patience brings perseverance, and perseverance brings hope, and hope is fulfilled in the love poured into our hearts by the Holy Spirit. The Holy Trinity reveals itself to us through our progress in the Christian life. As we are drawn more and more completely into the life of the Trinity, so our understanding becomes more and more developed.

Any child can learn, and no doubt should learn, that in the Holy Trinity we acknowledge three divine persons in one substance; but how much does that knowledge mean to the child? Not much, probably, and not much to us either if we do not progress beyond the elementary stage of our religion to the deep and comforting conviction that God is our Father. That is not simply some fact that we have learnt, but an utter certainty because the Spirit in the depths of our being calls out to him, 'Abba, Father;' and this is the key to the most important relationship in our lives, a relationship of total trust and confidence and dependence, as of children on their Father.

And to the conviction too that God the Son is one of us, has taken our nature into his; so that God is not simply 'up there' or 'out there' but here with us – Emmanuel, God with us, to use a traditional title of Jesus – sharing our hopes and fears, sharing our triumphs and our tragedies, knowing our sufferings and feeling our pain, walking with us on our journey.

And to the conviction that God the Spirit dwells in our hearts, leading us, as Jesus says, to the complete truth; and, moreover, changing us, transforming us, healing us, moulding us into the image of Christ, giving us growth in faith and hope and love; bearing, as Saint Paul says, united witness with our spirit that we are children of God; and if children, then heirs as well: heirs of God and co-heirs with Christ, sharing his sufferings so as to share his glory.

Corpus Christi
CORPUS CHRISTI

Readings
Gen 14:18-20; 1 Cor 11:23-26; Lk 9:11-17

Every year when I celebrate Trinity Sunday I ask myself why we need a special Sunday dedicated to the Blessed Trinity. Is there any God to worship, other than the Trinity? What are we worshipping every other Sunday of the year, if not the Trinity? Would it not be remarkable to have an Untrinity Sunday?

I ask myself a similar question a few days later, when we celebrate the feast of the Body and Blood of Christ. Is not every Mass a celebration of the Body and Blood of Christ? What else are we celebrating at the Mass, if not the Body and Blood of Christ? Would it not be remarkable to have a Mass where the bread and wine did *not* turn into the Body and Blood of Christ?

But familiarity can lead to contempt, or at least neglect of and indifference to, the Holy Sacrament, so it is salutary to pause and reflect what a great gift Jesus has given us in the Eucharist.

Jesus himself compares it with the manna given to the people of Israel in the desert. The Israelites, you will remember, had nothing to eat as they travelled through the wilderness, and in their hunger they cried out to God. And he sent them manna from above: a white substance, like snowflakes, which they gathered and ate. This was a remarkable thing, and a great sign of God's love for them. But they grew bored with it, and even complained about it. They longed for variety. They cried out: 'Who will give us meat to eat? Think of the fish we used to eat free in Egypt, the cucumbers, melons, leeks, onions and garlic! Here we are wasting away, stripped of everything; there is nothing but manna for us to look at!'

In rather the same way, Catholics sometimes get bored with Mass. I've heard people say it: 'It's always the same, week after week. Always the same thing!' And no doubt this is why so many people, especially younger people, fall away from attendance at Mass. Well, I suppose it is always the same thing. But what a thing! The Bread of Angels; the Living Bread come down from Heaven; the Hidden Manna; the Pledge of Glory; the Sacrament most Holy; the Word made Flesh; the Body of Christ.

The Ordinary Sundays
of the Year

The Baptism of Our Lord takes the place of
the First Sunday of the Year.

Second Sunday of the Year
GIFTS

Readings
Isa 62:1-5; 1 Cor 12:4-11; Jn 2:1-11

'There is a variety of gifts but always the same Spirit.' The truth of Saint Paul's statement is evident to anyone who is in any way involved in a parish church. In any parish you must have a priest, to say the Mass; but you will also have altar servers, readers, singers, organists and other musicians, eucharistic ministers, catechists, welcomers, secretaries of many organisations, cleaners and flower arrangers, those who count collections and keep the finances in order, those who make the tea, and, most important of all, those who support the whole edifice with their prayers and their financial contributions.

All are necessary parts of the body of Christ. Some are more obviously vital than others. Cut out the heart from a body, and the body will die very quickly. Cut out the kidneys or the spleen, and death may not be instantaneous, but the body *will* be impaired. Those parts are there for a reason.

I wonder what is *your* particular function in the Body of Christ? I'm sure you have one, and I'm sure it should be valued. I think of Saint Thérèse of Lisieux, how she heard two nuns talking about her through her window. 'Poor Thérèse,' they were saying. 'We all have our particular gifts, but Thérèse hasn't got any at all. She's no use to anyone.' Very hurtful words, and a terrible example of pride; but also untrue. Thérèse had the most valuable gift of all, the gift of love. In the Body of Christ, it was her vocation to be the heart.

So, don't let anybody put you down, and don't put yourself down. You are a unique and precious individual. You have very valuable gifts. What gifts do you have? Perhaps you are now of mature years. Your children have grown up, perhaps you are widowed. You have the gift of time. Perhaps some of that gift could be given back to God, some of that time could be used to pray for the needs of the parish, or to visit the sick. Perhaps you have have the gift of a good education. You can read clearly. That gift could be offered back to God as you proclaim his word in the liturgy.

Once we get into the way of offering our gifts back to God, wonderful things begin to happen. Think of the Gospel story of the feeding of the five thousand. The disciples have five loaves and two fishes; but what is that among so many? It seems pitifully inadequate, an insignificant gift to offer to God; but God takes it and transforms it and multiplies it in a wonderful way. Or think of what we do at the Mass. Somebody brings forward a few wafers of bread and a jug of very ordinary wine, to be offered to God. And what does God do with those gifts? He transforms them into the Body and Blood of his Son, they become the bread of life and the cup of everlasting salvation.

Or think of the Gospel story of the wedding at Cana in Galilee. They run out of wine, so what *do* they have to offer? Only water, a very common and humble substance. But Jesus transforms that very ordinary gift into something precious and glorious.

That transformation is a parable of what he is doing in us. We offer him our gifts: humble and ordinary they may seem, but he will transform them into something very special, into the glorious new wine of his kingdom. With *our* gifts, God can heal the sick, bring hope to the despairing, and salvation to those who seemed beyond redemption; with our gifts he can build up his kingdom, and hasten that day when the earth will be filled with the glory of God as the waters cover the sea.

Third Sunday of the Year
ANOINTED

Readings
Neh 8:2-6.8-10; 1 Cor 12:12-30; Lk 1:1-4.14-21

One of my earliest memories is of the coronation of Queen Elizabeth. We didn't have television in those days, but I saw a lot of the service in Pathé News at the cinema. I saw the golden coach, with the footmen walking in front. I saw the Archbishop of Canterbury placing the crown on the queen's head. One detail of the service I didn't see: the anointing. This was considered too holy for the public gaze, and was done under a canopy, so that even the people in the Abbey couldn't see it properly. But I remember my teacher in school explaining that the Archbishop poured oil on the queen's head. At that time my father had a particularly dirty oil can, which usually contained engine oil, and I had a fantasy of the Archbishop pouring such a can of Castrol over the queen. Even at the age of five, I thought it strange that such a gross custom should intrude itself into the dignity of the coronation service.

Now of course, I know better. The oil used is not Castrol, but olive oil, and the anointing, far from being a gross intrusion into the service, is the very heart of it, the act used to make kings and queens from the earliest times. Jesus takes Isaiah's words about anointing and applies them to himself: 'The spirit of the Lord has been given to me, for he has anointed me.' Jesus has been anointed king of a very special kingdom, a kingdom which offers good news to the poor, and liberty to captives, and sight to the blind, and freedom to the downtrodden.

We ourselves are citizens of that kingdom. More than that, we have ourselves been anointed as members of that royal priesthood, kings and priests in the Kingdom of God. What then are we doing to bring good news to the poor, to proclaim liberty to captives, and sight to the blind, and freedom to the downtrodden?

Sometimes we are apt to feel helpless, and even guilty, because it seems to us that we are not doing very much. We see homeless people, for example. Perhaps we give a homeless person some spare change. It must occur to us that we're not making much impression on the overall problem. The same is true when we hear of famines and disasters in the developing world. Most of us will have felt shame that we're doing so little to bring good news to the poor.

When we feel like this, the important thing to remember is that we are not simply isolated individuals. We are members of the body of Christ, each of us making our own contribution to the body. Not everybody can be a prophet, or an apostle, or a teacher, says Saint Paul. He might have said, that not everyone can be a development worker, or a missionary, or a worker with the homeless. But we can support those who are, by our giving, by our prayers, by our interest.

Let me give you a particular example. Some years ago a young man called Peter visited Colombia, in South America. He was horrified by the plight of the street children. These children – some of them orphans, some of them with very deprived home backgrounds – were living by begging and stealing, and sleeping in sewers. Some of them were under five years old. The local people regarded them as a nuisance and felt justified in killing them and throwing their bodies on rubbish-tips. Today Peter is a priest in Colombia, having founded a charity which provides shelter, food and clothing and education for those children. Not everyone can go to Colombia and do apostolic work of that kind; but everyone can support the work. Indeed the work could not go on without our support. And there are many other agencies of relief or development, many missionary societies, many groups which work for peace and justice for all, which rely on our prayers and contributions.

We are the body of Christ; individually we are its members, its eyes and limbs and ears. As individuals we can do little; but together, as the body of Christ, we can and will bring good news to the poor, proclaim liberty to captives, new sight to the blind, freedom to the downtrodden; we can and will proclaim the year of the Lord's favour.

Fourth Sunday of the Year
LOVE

Readings
Jer 1:4-5.17-19; 1 Cor 12:31–13:13; Lk 4:21-30

Love is always patient and kind: it is never jealous; love is never boastful or conceited; it is never rude or selfish; it does not take offence, and is not resentful. Love takes no pleasure in other people's sins but delights in the truth; it is always ready to excuse, to trust, to hope, and to endure whatever comes.

Paul offers us here a complete rule of life, and we could not do better than to write it out and hang it on the wall, to try to live by it day by day, to let it direct and inform all our relationships, to use it as an examination of conscience and to confess all our lapses from it. Let's spend a couple of minutes doing just that.

Love is always patient and kind. Are we always patient? Do we bear with the infirmities and follies of others, or must we always be first? Must everybody serve our needs? If we have to wait our turn, do we do it cheerfully, or do we fume and fuss? Are we always kind? Whatever the situation, do we think what we can do to edify, to be helpful? Or are we apt to be sarcastic, or belittling?

It is never jealous. But are we jealous? Are we content with what we have and what we are, or are we jealous of other people's popularity, other people's income, other people's gifts?

Love is never boastful or conceited. Are we ever boastful? Do we find the need to blow our own trumpet? Are we conceited? Do we have an inflated opinion of ourselves, or do we humbly reckon others to be better than ourselves? Of course, a lot of people reckon that others *are* better than themselves, but not in a humble way; rather, in an envious way, in a way that owes more to neurosis and inferiority complex than true Christian humility. Do we look hard for the good points in other people, for the evidence of God's grace working in them, and when we find those points rejoice like someone who has found a pearl of great price? Or do we look for bad points, for weaknesses? When a friend gains a promotion, do we rejoice? Or do we say, Why couldn't *I* have got that?

It is never rude or selfish. Are *we* ever rude? When we speak to someone, is our first thought whether what we have to say will be helpful and salutary to that person, or do we speak our mind, however it may affect anybody else? Do we put ourselves at the service of others, or is everything we do for the benefit of self?

It does not take offence, and is not resentful. Are we quick to take offence? Do we recognise that the other person may be under strains and pressures of which we know nothing? Do we remember how easy it is to say the wrong thing, or are we unforgiving when others do so? Do we bear resentment for years, eating away inside us?

Love takes no pleasure in other people's sins but delights in the truth. Do we take pleasure in other people's sins? Do we enjoy gossiping about other people's wrongdoings and follies? Do we delight in the truth, or are we content to listen to gossip, and pass it on?

It is always ready to excuse, to trust, to hope, and to endure whatever comes. Are we ready to excuse? We read that someone has got in trouble with the law, or had an affair. Do we tut-tut, and condemn? Or do we reflect that the person may have been under great strain, or subject to temptations which we, mercifully, are spared? Are we ready to trust? Or is our motto 'Once bitten, twice shy?' Are we ready to hope, or are we inclined to be negative – nothing good will come out of that, you're wasting your time? Are we ready to endure whatever comes, or do we have a low tolerance for things that need to be endured? Are we willing to serve Christ only if we can do so in comfort, without unduly disrupting our routine? Or, do we love?

Fifth Sunday of the Year
THE VISION OF GOD

Readings
Isa 6:1-6; 1 Cor 15:1-11; Lk 5:1-11

Why do we come to church? What do we hope to find here? Many good things, no doubt: companionship, fellowship, teaching, support, uplift. But surely, above all, we hope to find God: a glimpse of God, the God who made us and redeemed us, the God who loves us and whom we try our best to love. But if a vision of God were granted to us, could we bear it?

A Russian Orthodox bishop writes of a man who came to see him complaining that never in his life had he been granted any vision of God. The bishop asked him if there was any passage in the Bible which spoke to him particularly. The man said yes, he had always been moved by the story in the gospel of the woman taken in adultery. So the bishop asked where the man imagined himself in the story: was he the woman herself, was he Christ, declining to condemn her, was he one of those going away shamefaced because he knew that he was not himself without sin? The man replied no, he saw himself as the only one who would not have left, but would have stayed and put the woman to death. The bishop said, 'Then, thank God that he does *not* allow you to see him.'

How often have we had to thank God that he did *not* make his presence known to us? We read in the Bible of two men who came face to face with the living God, and found the experience more than they could bear. Isaiah sees the Lord, seated in all his glory on his throne, worshipped by the seraphim. Does the sight fill him with wonder, love and praise? It does not. It fills him with dread. He says, 'What a wretched state I am in! I am lost, for I am a man of unclean lips, and I live among a people of unclean lips, and my eyes have looked at the King, the Lord of hosts.'

God appears in a gentler form to Peter. Not now on his throne of glory, not now seated amid the cherubim and seraphim, God appears to Peter in the form of a man like himself. But Peter has the discernment to see the divinity in Jesus, concealed under the cloak of his humanity, and he falls to his knees saying, 'Leave me, Lord; I am a sinful man.'

And now, God in his gentleness and kindness shows himself to us in still gentler forms, in bread and wine, or in the persons of the sick, the needy or those in prison. He speaks to us, not in the deafening thunder of Sinai, but in the words of the Scriptures. He does not impose his presence on us in a way that would crush and destroy us. He comes to us so gently that often we may fail to see him at all. Sometimes we hear of one of the saints being granted a more direct vision of God; and we may envy such a vision. But are we ready for it?

Our whole Christian life is a process of being made ready for that vision, for heaven is nothing less that the vision of God, face to face; and lasting, not for a fleeting moment, but through all eternity. Now we see through a glass, darkly, in shadows. But those glimpses of God, in the sacraments, in the sick and the poor, train our eyes for the more perfect vision of God. When God knows that we are ready, we shall see him face to face, and rejoice in the unmediated splendour of the eternal glory of the Lord of Hosts.

Sixth Sunday of the Year
FOR THIS LIFE ONLY

Readings
Jer 17:5-8; 1 Cor 15:12.16-20; Lk 6:17.20-26

I once read in one of our Catholic papers a sad letter from a man who said he couldn't believe in a loving God because his wife had died in great pain. When we hear of suffering and disappointment and pain the best response is to offer comfort and healing, rather than a sermon; but I couldn't help reflecting that this unhappy man could not have received a very sound formation in the faith.

We do not believe, and it is no part of God's promises to us, that if we live a good life we shall be free from suffering and illness and bereavement. These things are part of life, and we are not exempt from them. In fact, in some ways Christians attract suffering: that is part of our vocation. Nor does God promise long life, prosperity, earthly happiness, success, fame, honour, respect, security or comfort to his children. Saint Paul tells us that if our hope in Christ has been for this life only, we are the most unfortunate of all people. Because at that level, Christ simply does not deliver.

What he does deliver, he himself makes clear in the Gospel:

How happy are you who are poor; yours is the kingdom of God. Happy you who are hungry now: you shall be satisfied. Happy you who weep now: you shall laugh. Happy are you when people hate you, drive you out, abuse you, denounce your name as criminal, on account of the Son of Man. Rejoice when that day comes and dance for joy, for then your reward will be great in heaven.

Our reward does not come in this world. This world lasts but a brief time; our particular stake in it lasts a mere threescore years and ten, or at the most a century. The world to come is eternal, and we are promised nothing less than eternal, unending bliss, the unclouded vision of God himself, our Creator and Father; the company of the blessed saints and of the angels. There we shall meet face to face with Christ our Saviour and Lord – crucified, risen, ascended and glorified. There he will wipe every tear from our eye. There we shall meet his blessed mother, who has so often prayed to her Son on our behalf.

The beauty and the glory and the wonder of the world to come surpasses our ability to express it, so we fall back on the words of the Apostle: 'I consider that the sufferings of this present time are not worth comparing with the glory that is to be revealed to us.' Or we have recourse to the splendid vision of Saint John the Divine:

> I heard a loud voice from the throne saying, Behold, the dwelling of God is with men. He will dwell with them, and they shall be his people, and God himself will be with them; he will wipe away every tear from their eyes, and death shall be no more, neither shall there be mourning nor crying nor pain any more, for the former things have passed away.

Seventh Sunday of the Year
LOVE YOUR ENEMIES

Readings
1 Sam 26:2.7-9.12-13.22-23; 1 Cor 15:45-49; Lk 6:27-38

'Love your enemies.' The Gospel presents us with Christ's most characteristic teaching. Christ himself practised what he preached. He did indeed bless those who cursed him, he prayed for forgiveness for those who crucified him. Those who follow this teaching most closely are most entitled to call themselves followers of Christ. If we look at our own behaviour and compare it with the teaching of Christ, how well do we measure up?

Do we love our enemies? Or do we nurse a hatred for those who have upset us? Do we always love even those who love us, or do we take them for granted, or find fault with them? Do we do good to those who hate us? Or do we, on the contrary, do badly to those who love us? Do we bless those who curse us? Or do we curse them back? Do we even curse those who bless us?

What do we do about those who slap us on the cheek? Do we slap them back harder? Do we give to everyone who asks from us? Or do we find excuses not to give? Do we treat others as we would like them to treat us? How, actually, would we like others to treat us? I'm always grateful when people realise that I can't always be at my best, that I may have worries and anxieties of my own. No doubt you too are grateful when people make allowances for you. Do we always make allowances for others? If people are grumpy or bad-tempered, do we reflect that they may have worries and stresses about which we know nothing, or do we snap back at them?

Are we compassionate as our Father is compassionate? Or do we demand our pound of flesh? Do we judge? Do we condemn? These are very dangerous things to do. As a prison chaplain, I often had cause to reflect how fallible human judgement can be. Our religion centres on the worship of a man who was wrongly condemned to death. What makes us confident that our own judgement is just?

Are we ready to grant pardon? Pardon is at the heart of the Christian life. Christ pronounced our pardon on the cross. We bring our sins to the priest and hear those wonderful words, 'Go in peace, the Lord has freed you from your sins.' What words could make us happier? But how ready are we to say them to others?

'Give,' says Jesus, 'and there will be gifts for you: a full measure, pressed down, shaken together, and running over, will be poured into your lap; because the amount you measure out is the amount you will be given back.' So how much shall we measure out? How much shall we give? How much of our time, how much of our concern, how much of our love? Shall we give without measure? Because if we do, we shall be children of the Most High, for he himself is kind to the ungrateful and the wicked.

Eighth Sunday of the Year
THE BLIND LEADING THE BLIND

Readings
Ecclus 27:4-7; 1 Cor 15:54-58; Lk 6:39-45

There is a well-known painting by Peter Breughel, illustrating our Lord's saying about the blind leading the blind. It shows a line of six blind men. The first has already fallen into a pond, the second is in the process of falling after him, and the other four are about to follow them. In the background is a church. I don't know whether Breughel understood the story as a parable of the Church, with the loyal followers following their blind teachers to perdition. Certainly Jesus directed the saying against the religious authorities of his own day; clearly he didn't think they were up to much.

We, however, don't read the Scriptures simply to discover how unsatisfactory the religious teachers were in our Lord's day. We need to apply his teaching to our own day. Are *we* being led up the garden path and into the garden pond? And I need to ask myself very carefully whether, as a pastor, I am leading my flock along the safe path to the green pastures, or whether, on the contrary, I am leading you over a cliff.

In Breughel's picture, each of those blind men is utterly dependent on the one in front, and if he falls into a ditch, the others have no alternative but to follow. We, however, are not in quite so desperate a situation. Each of us is in the happy position of being able to keep our own eyes open. That is to say, we can think for ourselves, and inform ourselves, about the safe path to salvation. I'm not saying for a moment that anyone should abandon the teaching and guidance of the Church. But we can receive that teaching more effectively and intelligently if we take the trouble to inform ourselves about our faith.

For example, I would regard it as part of every Catholic's religious duty to read the Bible frequently, to be familiar with it, to know it and love it. All too often it can seem a strange and alien book. And yet I think of some words of the Psalmist:

> Your word is a lamp for my steps
> and a light for my path.

Surely anyone familiar with the Bible possesses a sure guide through the dangerous pathways of life. On the other hand, if we do not know the Bible, we have, in the words of Jesus, a great plank in our eye. How shall we see our own way to salvation, let alone guide others along the right path?

Saint Paul tells us, in his letter to Timothy, that from the Scriptures we can learn the wisdom that leads to salvation through faith in Christ Jesus. All Scripture, he tells us, is inspired by God and can profitably be used for teaching, for refuting error, for guiding people's lives and teaching them to be holy. 'Teaching, refuting error, guiding people's lives and teaching them to be holy' – that must constitute a large part of what Paul urges us to do today, when he tells us to keep on working at the Lord's work always. We cannot do this without a thorough knowledge of the Scriptures.

So once again I would recommend the frequent, indeed daily, reading of the Bible so that we may become what Jesus calls fully trained disciples, like their teacher, that is like Jesus himself.

Ninth Sunday of the Year
THE CENTURION

Readings
1 Kgs 8:41-43; Gal 1:1-2.6-10; Lk 7:1-10

A centurion was a non-commissioned officer; he had come up through the ranks. He was in charge of a hundred men, so he would be roughly equivalent to a company sergeant major. As an enlisted soldier, he would have learnt how to take orders; the Roman army had a short way with those who did not obey orders. As a centurion, he would have learnt how to *give* orders; to this day, when the sergeant major tells the men to jump, they jump, and they don't come down till he tells them. His training told him that Jesus didn't need to walk across the village to deal personally with a little thing like a sick servant; officers didn't put themselves to that trouble. One order, one word of command, would suffice.

Do *we* have the right training? Has our Christian formation taught us that Jesus has all authority in heaven and earth given to him? Do we really trust him? The Church believes that Jesus is the Christ, the Son of the Living God. But who do *I* think that he is? Do I really believe, as the centurion did, that he is the commander, the King, the Lord?

The centurion would have undergone a long and arduous military training. What sort of training must we receive in order to trust Jesus as the centurion did? There is a training which Christians must undergo; it is often referred to in the New Testament. Saint Paul sometimes compares Christian discipleship with the training to which an athlete must subject himself if he is to stand a chance of winning:

> All the runners at the stadium are trying to win, but only one of them gets the prize. You must run in the same way, meaning to win. All the fighters at the games go into strict training; they do this just to win a wreath that will wither away, but we do it for a wreath that will never wither. That is how I run, intent on winning; that is how I fight, not beating the air. I treat my body hard and make it obey me.

That is the way the martyrs of old found the courage and strength to follow Christ even to the point of death. That is the way in which Christians in many parts of the world even today, are finding the courage to lay down their lives for Christ. If we in this part of the world are not achieving much, if we find that our numbers are dwindling, and the number of our priests is declining almost to vanishing-point, it is perhaps because we have lost some of that discipline. Perhaps we never received an adequate training, or perhaps we have ceased to practise it.

What goes into a Christian's training? First of all, a determination to be present at Mass every Sunday, however difficult that may be. Then, regularity at prayer. We should not turn off the light at night without having prayed during the day. All priests, and a growing number of lay people, say the daily office, or at least part of it. It's not a bad idea to have a copy of Night Prayer on the bedside table, so that even if we've said nothing else to God during the day, we need not close our eyes on a prayerless day. Then, most Catholics can say the Rosary, and if any have given up the practice, it may be a good idea to take it up again. A Christian's training should include a regular examination of conscience, and Confession when necessary; and, though there's very little emphasis on it nowadays, it should include fasting.

One thing I've left to last, and that is Bible-reading. Catholics sometimes think this is not necessary. But of course it is. We will not know Christ unless we have read about him in the Gospels, and if we do not know him, we will not trust him, and if we do not trust him, our prayer to him will be a feeble and half-hearted thing. Reading the Scriptures – and not only the Gospels, for all the Scriptures refer to Christ in some way – is an essential part of Christian discipleship. If we make the reading of the Bible our daily habit, that, more than anything, will instill in us the faith which Jesus commended in the centurion of Capernaum.

Tenth Sunday of the Year
RAISED TO NEW LIFE

Readings
1 Kgs 17:17-24; Gal 1:11-19; Lk 7:11-17

We read of two great miracles today: two young men are raised from the dead. Elijah raises a dead boy to life and restores him to his mother, and Jesus raises to life the son of the widow of Nain. In neither case are we told anything about the subsequent life of the young man raised from the dead. These men were given a second chance; I should be very interested to know what they did for the rest of their new lives. If *I* were given a second chance, if *I* were raised to a new life, I think I might live it very differently from the way I have lived this one.

But what am I saying? I *have* been given a second chance, I *have* been given a new life, I *have* been born again, and so have you, in the mystery of Baptism. The trouble is, that most of us were baptised at such an early age that the new life is the only life we have known. We regard it as normal, natural, ordinary. How different it was for Saint Paul: halfway through his natural life he was called by God to a new life, and given an entirely new direction. As he says, 'God, who had specially chosen me while I was still in my mother's womb, called my through his grace and chose to reveal his Son in me.' God chose each of us specially while we were in our mother's womb; but in most cases, we were hardly out of our mother's womb before being raised to the new life in Baptism.

We are none the less special, none the less called through God's grace, none the less chosen to reveal his Son in us. Each of us can say, no less than Saint Paul, 'I have been crucified with Christ, and I live now, not with my own life but with the life of Christ who lives in me.'

What are we going to do with this life of Christ who lives in us? What an impact Saint Paul made on the world by living with the life of Christ who lived in him! What an impact did so many of the saints make, living that same life! What a phenomenal impact the Church would make, if every one of its members – you and I and every other Christian in the world – were to live, not with our own life but with the life of Christ who lives in us. Then would come about the new Jerusalem, of which it is said:

Here God lives among men. He will make his home among them; they shall be his people, and he will be their God; his name is God-with-them. He will wipe away all tears from their eyes; there will be no more death, and no more mourning or sadness. The world of the past has gone.

Eleventh Sunday of the Year
YOUR SINS ARE FORGIVEN

Readings
2 Sam 12:7-10.13; Gal 2:16.19-21; Lk 7:36–8:3

Our readings show us two remarkable examples of forgiveness. Let us remind ourselves of the enormity of David's sin. He had coveted the wife of his neighbour, Uriah the Hittite, thus breaking the ninth commandment; he had committed adultery with her, thus breaking the sixth; to cover up the scandal, he had arranged for Uriah to be killed, thus breaking the fifth. The vileness of his actions was compounded by the fact that Uriah had been David's loyal subject, fighting in David's army against David's enemies. Yet David had only to acknowledge his sin to have it forgiven: David said to Nathan, 'I have sinned against the Lord.' Then Nathan said to David, 'The Lord, for his part, forgives your sin.'

You might think that God dispensed his forgiveness pretty cheaply, but it wasn't as cheap as all that. The child whom David had begotten on Uriah's wife would die. That was a heavy price for David to pay, and not only for David: the child was innocent.

Why should it be the one to pay the price of David's sin? But it is characteristic of sin that the innocent get hurt. We have seen how, in the conflict between Israel and Gaza, most of those who suffered were civilians, many of them children. Why can those who have a quarrel not settle it between themselves, without bringing undeserved suffering on the innocent? Alas, it's not possible. We are so bound together that, when one person is hurt, many others are hurt with him. Someone robs a post office, and in so doing shoots the postmaster. The postmaster is killed, his wife is widowed, his children orphaned, and all his family and friends grief-stricken and traumatized. The robber is put in prison, quite rightly – but now *his* wife and children are ruined, his parents are shamed, his friends are shocked, and the ripples caused by his sin continue to spread outward.

It might seem that a quite different set of rules applies to the woman who had sinned in the Gospel. Jesus tells her, 'Your sins are forgiven. Your faith has saved you: go in peace' There is no mention of a price to be paid, of a child who has to die, of any ill-effect whatever resulting from her sin. And yet, there is a heavy price to be paid, not by the woman, not by her children or family, but by Jesus himself. Jesus volunteers to pay the inevitable price of her sins, and of the sins of all the world, to pay it in his agony and bloody sweat, in the marks of the lash, in his bearing of the crown of thorns, in the spittle on his face, in the wounds in his hands and feet and side. 'Let me bear this for you,' he says. 'For your part, go in peace: your sins are forgiven.' As it is written in the book of the prophet Isaiah:

> Ours were the sufferings he bore, ours the sorrows he carried. But we, we thought of him as someone punished, struck by God, and brought low. Yet he was pierced through for our faults, crushed for our sins. On him lies a punishment that brings us peace, and through his wounds we are healed.

Twelfth Sunday of the Year
TAKE UP YOUR CROSS

Readings
Zech 12:10-11; 13:1; Gal 3:26-29; Lk 9:18-24

'If anyone wants to be a follower of mine,' says Jesus, 'let him renounce himself and take up his cross every day and follow me.' This is one of the hardest sayings of Jesus, but also one of the most familiar. Everyone knows, or should know, that if you want to be a follower of Jesus you will have to bear a cross, as he did. If you were brought into the Church without having this important truth explained to you, please collect your refund at the door. But I cannot believe that many people have followed

Christ for long without realising that there is a cross to be borne. He tells us so, not only in this passage, but in many other places in the Gospel.

Note that Jesus says that anyone who wants to follow him must take up *his* cross; not just any cross, but your own particular cross. We all have our cross to bear, but we don't all have to bear the same cross. Your cross may be very different from mine. Some may have to bear the cross of sickness, others the cross of bereavement, others the cross of loneliness or of humiliation or of poverty or of unpopularity or of injury. You know best the name of the cross you have to bear.

Nobody likes to bear a cross: a cross is a heavy and a cruel thing. We would all like to put down our cross, and walk away from it. But to bear a cross in fellowship with Jesus is to help him in his grand scheme for the redemption of the world. If we give up our life for the sake of the Gospel, we shall save our life. If we cast away our cross, we cast away our crown. Saint Paul, who more than anyone shared in the cross of Christ so as to share in his glory, writes: 'It makes me happy to suffer for you, as I am suffering now, and in my own body to do what I can to make up all that has still to be undergone by Christ for his body, the Church.'

Despite the words of Paul, it does not usually make us happy to suffer, and we find it hard to understand how bearing our cross can achieve any positive result. This is because we cannot see through the veil that separates this world from the next, and comprehend the majesty of God's plan. We see well enough the miseries that litter this vale of tears: the wars, the injustice, the sickness, the poverty, the squalor, the inhumanity. We cannot yet see the glory, that glory of which Paul says 'I think that what we suffer in this life can never be compared to the glory, as yet unrevealed, which is waiting for us.'

To bear the cross to the end is to ensure not only our own glory, but the glory of countless millions whom we do not even know. So again, Paul says, 'I bear it all for the sake of those who are chosen, so that in the end they may have the salvation that is in Christ Jesus and the eternal glory that comes with it.'

Thirteenth Sunday of the Year
SPREAD THE NEWS

Readings
1 Kgs 19:16.19-21; Gal 5:1.13-18; Lk 9:51-62

'Leave the dead to bury their dead,' says Jesus; 'Your duty is to go and spread the news of the kingdom of God.' What if Jesus were to say such a thing to us? I don't mean the bit about leaving the dead to bury their dead, but the great commission which follows: 'Your duty is to go and spread the news of the kingdom of God.' Of course, Jesus does say exactly that to us. It is the duty of every Christian to go and spread the news of the kingdom of God.

How do we spread that good news? There are many ways to do so: by our example, by our prayers, by our giving. Saint Francis once famously said that we must spread the Gospel by every means, even using words if necessary.

And sometimes words *are* necessary. We should be prepared to give an account of our hope. This need not be confrontational. If we are bearing witness to our faith by our actions, even to the extent of coming regularly to Mass, there will be occasions when friends and other people of goodwill are going to ask us what we believe in, and why. They are, we may assume, not trying to ridicule us but are genuinely interested in this good news, and perhaps even hope to be convinced by it, so that they may share in the joy and the hope which they see we possess. It would be a pity not to take advantage of such a God-given opportunity. So we need to be able to put the good news into words. What shall we say to such an enquirer?

We could, and I think we should, tell such a person the story of how God, the Creator of heaven and earth, sent his Son into the world to offer its citizens the chance of eternal life; of how he taught them the most sublime lessons concerning love, forgiveness, and the hope of everlasting blessedness; how he was rejected and killed, but on the third day rose from the dead, showing the infinite power he wielded over life and death; how, in the sight of his disciples, he ascended into heaven; how he sent his Holy Spirit upon them, filling them with confidence and power. How he sustains his people now, washing away their sins in Baptism and strengthening them with his own body and blood in the Eucharist; how he sends his angels to watch over them and supports them through the prayers of the saints; how he promises them an eternity of bliss in the contemplation of the angels and saints, and, far above them, of God himself, 'the love that moves the sun and the other stars'.

No doubt that little account of the good news leaves much unsaid; there are i's to be dotted and t's to be crossed. But I think, if we told such a story, we would have made a good first step in fulfilling our Lord's command to go and spread the news of the Kingdom of God.

Fourteenth Sunday of the Year
SEVENTY-TWO OTHERS

Readings
Isa 66:10-14; Gal 6:14-18; Lk 10:1-12.17-20

How many men did Jesus call to be his apostles? Everybody knows that: there were twelve of them. And how many of them could you name? Peter and James and John, Andrew, Judas Iscariot, the other Judas, Philip, Thomas (struggling a bit now), the other James, the other Simon, Matthew, Bartholomew – why, that's all twelve. Most of their names are familiar. I dare say anybody could remember at least half of them without much difficulty.

But on another occasion, we read today, Jesus called another seventy-two to be his disciples. How many of *those* could you name? I don't think we know the names of any of them. Unlike the apostles, they are a quite anonymous group. And yet they were important people. They were entrusted with a very important mission: to proclaim that the kingdom of God was near at hand. They were given power to tread underfoot serpents and scorpions and the whole strength of the enemy. Even the devils submitted to them when they used the name of Jesus. Best of all, their names were written in heaven.

These seventy-two others were the first batch of those countless millions of people whom Jesus is still calling to do his work on earth. I like to think that those seventy-two stand for me and for my brother priests. In our diocese at least, there are not as many priests as there are parishes; and besides parishes, there are hospital chaplaincies, prison chaplaincies, school, college and university chaplaincies. We have our work cut out. Our situation is very like that of those first seventy-two: Jesus tells them, 'The harvest is rich, but the labourers are few, so ask the Lord of the harvest to send labourers to his harvest.' That much we *can* do.

And our anxiety to help with the harvest mustn't end with praying for vocations. We must ask what we ourselves can do. Often when you speak to people about the crisis in vocations they tell you what 'they' should do: that is, what the bishops should do, or what the Vatican should do, or what the pope should do. *They* should ordain married men, *they* should let priests get married, *they* should ordain women, *they* should bring priests from overseas, and so on. This really isn't very helpful.

What *is* helpful is when each one of us starts to ask, 'There's a shortage of priests. The harvest is rich, but the labourers are few. What can *I* do to help?' If we get out of the habit of thinking that the crisis in vocations is somebody else's problem, if every member of the Church responds to the need by saying 'Here I am, Lord, send *me*' – then I think the Church will go from strength to strength, and what seemed a crisis will be seen to be an opportunity to respond to God's call in a new and exciting way.

We can't all be priests, but there *is* something each one of us can do. The Church needs readers, eucharistic ministers, catechists, teachers, deacons, administrators, singers, organists, altar servers, fundraisers, cleaners, flower arrangers, visitors. There are so many ministries, so much that needs to be done. Perhaps we should think of those seventy-two others as representing seventy-two ministries *other* than that of priest. I'm sure there are at least seventy-two other things which need to be done.

If all of us, in our different ministries, collaborate, work together like the different parts of the one body, then we shall be a very powerful instrument to do God's work, and to build up his kingdom on earth.

Fifteenth Sunday of the Year
THE EARLY SAMARITAN

Readings
Deut 30:10-14; Col 1:15-20; Lk 10:25-37

Would you be the good Samaritan, who helped the man who had fallen among thieves, or would you be the priest or levite, who passed by on the other side of the road? Of course, you'd be the Samaritan. Nobody would be so callous as to leave that poor man to die.

But suppose the circumstances were just a little different. Let's suppose that you *are* that Samaritan. Your name is Ishmael ben Ephraim, and you are riding on your donkey, along the road from Jerusalem to Jericho. You come round the bend in the road and see the poor man who has fallen among thieves. Unfortunately, though, you've arrived just half an hour too early. The attack is still going on. The man is, at this very moment, being beaten up by a gang of ruffians, all armed to the teeth. What do you do? Do you intervene on behalf of that man, or do you wait discreetly, some way off, until they've finished their evil work? If you do intervene, you are likely to suffer the same fate as the man you want to help. But can you stand by and do nothing?

The thing is, you see, that you and I *are* that Samaritan who came too early. The world is full of people who have fallen among thieves, and are even now being robbed. There are those, for example, who are being crippled and robbed by debts which are not of their making, victims of economic policies which are not of their devising. When we see those horrendous pictures on television of people suffering famine, war, oppression, we need to reflect that these things are not happening by accident. Nor are they some punishment meted out by God. These things are caused by human beings, these people have in a very real sense fallen among thieves. But who are the thieves?

Perhaps we don't want to know who the thieves are. We would rather not know whose policies are causing this distress, whether or not our government is supporting some despotic regime because they buy our guns or our missiles, whether or not the bank where we deposit *our* savings is also acting as a loan shark in the third world. We don't want to get involved with the thieves. What we really want to do is what the Samaritan did, give the innkeeper a couple of coins and tell him to get on with it. But is that enough? Archbishop Helder Camara once famously said, 'When I give money to the poor, they call me a saint. When I ask why people *are* poor, they call me a communist.' All of us want to help the poor: we contribute generously to agencies devoted to the relief of suffering. But how many of us take the time to read the literature from those agencies explaining the causes of that suffering? When did we last go to a talk or lecture about Third World debt? When did we last watch a television documentary on the subject?

These are uncomfortable, perhaps even painful matters. But if we stand aside from them, we are in effect standing aside while the robbers beat up the unfortunate man, and saying to them, 'Let us know when you've done beating up that poor fellow, because when you're done, we want to help him.'

Sixteenth Sunday of the Year
MARTHA AND MARY

Readings
Gen 18:1-10; Col 1:24-28; Lk 10:38-42

Which would you prefer to be, Martha, cumbered about with much serving, or Mary, choosing the better part, the one thing needful? Put like that, the question answers itself. We would all, I dare say, prefer to be Mary, sitting at the feet of the Lord. But chance would be a fine thing. We all have our necessary work to do. Some of us have to work for a living, some of us have to bring up children, some of us have to clean houses and cook meals. We are all, to some extent, cumbered about with much serving. Where are we going to find the time to sit at the feet of Jesus and listen to his teaching?

I wonder, though, if we really are as busy as we make out. I think of my mother, when I was a young boy. Almost every day she had to go shopping; there was no frozen food which you could store indefinitely. Every week she had to spend the best part of a day washing the laundry by hand; we had no washing machine. And there were many other chores, both for men and for women, which took a deal of time out of the week, and which are now done by machines. How are we using the time saved? Are we sitting at the feet of Jesus? Probably not. We find other jobs to do, and end up just as busy as before. Many people, after they retire, wonder how they ever found time to do a job.

Work, or at least keeping busy, can become a sort of idol. We don't feel that we've justified our existence unless we've been busy. Perhaps we need to remind ourselves that the ultimate good is not work, but rest.

The blessed souls in heaven are described as resting from their labours. God is said to have blessed the seventh day because on that day he rested from all *his* labours. Work, on the other hand, is described in the Bible as a curse imposed upon mankind as punishment for disobeying God's commandment.

Have we got work and rest the wrong way round in our scale of values? We would all agree that we need to rest in order to return, refreshed, to our work. If we didn't take some rest, the quality of our work would suffer, and so we agree that rest is necessary. But isn't that putting the cart before the horse? Surely we work in order to be able to enjoy our rest. If we didn't work, we wouldn't be able to afford a very comfortable rest.

But it is the rest which is the object of the exercise. So many people are in the tragic situation that they are working all the hours God sends to be able to afford a mortgage and a car and decent clothes, but they are so busy that they haven't the time to enjoy these good things.

Several times in the New Testament Jesus calls his disciples away from their work to enjoy a rest. For example, in Saint Mark's Gospel he says to them, 'Come away by yourselves to a lonely place, and rest a while.' For many were coming and going, and they had no leisure even to eat. And they went away in the boat to a lonely place by themselves.

We do well to follow their example: to get away from the hustle and bustle, to give ourselves space to think our own thoughts, and to reflect on the teachings of our Lord. Saint Paul writes to us about the mystery of Christ among us, our hope of glory. If we don't take that time for quiet reflection we will have very little sense that Christ *is* among us, and consequently very little hope of glory.

People fall away from the Church because, they say, they have lost their faith. You're bound to lose your faith if you don't give it space to grow, and yourself space to reflect on it and draw strength from it. But if we do give ourselves time to meditate on the sublime teachings and the wonderful promises of our Lord, then we will have chosen the better part, and it will not be taken away from us.

Seventeenth Sunday of the Year
GIVE US OUR DAILY BREAD

Readings
Gen 18:1-10; Col 2:12-14; Lk 11:1-13

Our Gospel reading offers us Saint Luke's version of the Lord's Prayer. We may notice that it is shorter than the version of Saint Matthew, which is the one we usually use in our prayers. Luke does not mention the petion 'Thy will be done, on earth as it is in heaven.' Nor does he mention the concluding petition, 'But deliver us from evil.'

Matthew focuses our attention on the petition, 'Forgive us our trespasses, as we forgive those who trespass against us.' He does this by having Jesus continue with the comment, 'Yes, if you forgive others their failings, your heavenly Father will forgive you yours; but if you do not forgive others, your Father will not forgive your failings either.'

Luke does not have this saying, but instead focuses on the petition, 'Give us each day our daily bread.' He has Jesus continue with the story of the man who goes knocking at his neighbour's door in the middle of the night, asking for bread; and, again, he has Jesus tell us that no father would give his son a stone when he asked for bread, or a snake when he asked for a fish, or a scorpion when he asked for an egg. For Luke, the Lord's Prayer is predominantly an appeal to our heavenly Father, not for forgiveness, but for our daily bread, that is, for the necessities of life. It is a confident appeal, for our Father will not refuse us. We have only to ask, and what we need will be given to us, we have only to knock, and the door will be opened to us.

It's an interesting critical question, whether Matthew or Luke more accurately reflects the intentions of Jesus himself. No doubt, Jesus intended that we should ask both for forgiveness and for the necessities of life. But as our liturgy today invites us to meditate on Luke's version, let us consider the implications of Luke's emphasis. Note that he says 'Give us each day' rather than 'Give us this day.' Each day of our life, today and tomorrow and the day after, we should look to God our heavenly Father to provide all our needs. It must be the characteristic of a Christian to live in complete dependency on God. And this dependency should not be a matter of anxiety: our heavenly Father will give us what we need, he will not let us down.

In fact, the petition is the antidote to anxiety. Fear not, says Jesus, as he says so often in Luke's Gospel. You have no need to be afraid, for your heavenly Father is looking after you. We find this confidence expressed even, or perhaps especially, in Luke's account of the crucifixion. In Matthew's Gospel, Jesus says only one thing on the cross: *Eli, Eli, lama sabachthani*; that is, 'My God, my God, why have you deserted me?' Matthew has Jesus experience the utter desolation of thinking that his Father has forsaken him. Luke does not subject Jesus to that degree of desolation, indeed to any feeling at all of desolation. Rather, he has Jesus carry on doing his Father's work, right up to the moment of death. As he is nailed to the cross, he says, 'Father, forgive them; they do not know what they are doing.' He has Jesus performing his great work of reconciling sinners to the Father, even as he is being crucified. Then he says to the repentant thief, 'Today you will be with me in paradise,' offering the thief the promise of forgiveness and a place among the blessed. Finally, he says, 'Father, into your hands I commit my spirit.' Far from being in an agony of desolation, he calmly entrusts his spirit to his Father, as he had entrusted every moment of his life to him.

Again, it's an interesting critical question, which evangelist offers us a more accurate account of the crucifixion. Probably neither of them sought to offer an exact historical account. Each tried to interpret the death of Jesus according to the principle he found most striking in his life and teaching. And for Luke, that principle was that God is our loving Father, who always hears our prayer, and will never let us down, even when the world is doing its worst. We should never lose confidence in him. It's a good principle, and we would do well to live by it.

Eighteenth Sunday of the Year
BIGGER BARNS

Readings
Eccles 1:2; 2:21-23; Col 3:1-5.9-11; Lk 12:13-21

To all appearances, the man in the story has been blessed by God. He is rich, he has enjoyed a good harvest, he has the means to take things easy, eat, drink and have a good time. Most of us would like to enjoy his good fortune; in fact, most of us act just as he did. We spend our working lives planning for a happy retirement. We pay off our mortgages, buy our retirement homes, ensure we have a decent pension. No harm in all that; it's normal behaviour, prudent behaviour, responsible behaviour. And yet the man in the story is called a fool. That hurts, because that man is just like us. Why is he a fool?

Because this life does not go on for ever. He could die tonight, and then what would be the benefit of all his toil, all his planning, all his prudence? Even so, you might say, he was no fool. Even if life is short, why not enjoy however much of it is granted to us? What's wrong with enjoying plenty of good things, taking things easy, eating and drinking the good things God gives us, having a good time as long as it lasts? Nothing, so long as we do not forget that there is another life which is not short, which is not only longer, but infinitely longer, than this brief life on earth.

That is why Jesus, again and again, urges us to store up treasure, not on earth, but in heaven; for where our treasure is, there our hearts will be. And our hearts need to be set, not on things that are on the earth, but on heavenly things. It may be harder nowadays than it was in the past, to set our thoughts on heavenly things, because our imaginations are stimulated in so many ways, by films, by television, increasingly by the internet. These media stimulate our minds to think, not about heavenly things, but very definitely about things that are on the earth: new cars, attractive clothes, things that look nice, things that taste nice, things that smell nice.

The attractions of heaven may seem a bit remote, a bit theo-
retical, in comparison with the attractions offered to us by our
television screens.

Perhaps we should have a real campaign to stimulate our
imaginations with images of heaven. There are enough of them
in the Bible. Saint Paul writes, 'I think that what we suffer in this
life can never be compared to the glory, as yet unrevealed, which
is waiting for us.' Our Lord himself describes the kingdom of
heaven as a pearl of great price, as treasure hidden in a field, as
something worth far more than all that this world has to offer.
It would be good to read these things often, to have our imaginations stirred to strive to gain that hidden treasure.

Reading the New Testament is an excellent thing, but it's not
the only way to stimulate our imaginations. We are accustomed
to look at images on screens, whether of cars, clothes, food, or
beautiful people. We are tempted by the lust of the eyes. But we
can turn that to our advantage. We can feed our imaginations
with images of heaven. Unfortunately, there is often very little
in a modern Catholic church to stimulate the visual imagination; sometimes no more than a few tacky statues. I'm looking
forward to going on holiday in my beloved Crete where there
are churches decorated from end to end with images of heaven.
For a couple of weeks I shall be gazing at images of the saints
in glory, of our Lord himself in majesty, surrounded by his holy
angels. That's the stuff to stir the imagination and fill our hearts
with longing for the courts of heaven.

Sight is not the only sense. It's helpful also to fill our ears with
the sounds of heaven. The finest music that the world has ever
known has been composed to the glory of God. The Masses of
Palestrina and Byrd, of Mozart and Haydn, are some of the greatest evocations imaginable of the glory of heaven. And it's easier
than ever to listen to them. Someone may say that the liturgical
music of the past was much better than that of today. Maybe so,
but it the past very few churches had the resources to perform

that music. Nowadays we can all listen to it in our living rooms, in our cars, even as we walk around town.

Manufacturers of cars, clothes, furniture and every sort of commodity are trying to fill our minds with images of their products, to encourage us to buy them. Why shouldn't we fill our minds, our hearts, our imaginations, with images of heaven, and so be motivated to purchase that pearl of great price?

Nineteenth Sunday of the Year
BE READY

Readings
Wis 18:6-9; Heb 11:1-2.8-19; Lk 12:32-48

Saint Philip was standing by the roadside when a chariot drove by. In the chariot was a man reading from the prophet Isaiah. Philip could hear what he was reading, because the custom in those days was to read aloud. Immediately Philip asked him, 'Do you understand what you are reading?' The man asked Philip to get into the chariot and explain it to him; and when Philip had told him about the death and resurrection of Jesus, the man was baptised, so becoming the first Ethiopian Christian.

Can you imagine how alert, how ready for action, Saint Philip must have been? A chariot comes past. Philip hears a few words. He has only a second to act; the chariot is moving; another second and it will be past. If you or I had been at the roadside, no doubt we would have said, 'What that man was reading sounded very interesting. It would have been good to have had a word with him about it.' But we would have missed the opportunity. Philip did not miss the opportunity, and because of his alertness salvation came to the man in the chariot, and a whole new country was opened up to the Gospel.

Jesus tells us to be alert. 'See that you are dressed for action and have your lamps lit. Be like men waiting for their master to return from the wedding feast, ready to open the door as soon as he comes and knocks.'

I do not think we should interpret that too narrowly as referring only to our Lord's final coming at the end of time. You might think that Christ has kept the Church for a long time on the edge of its seat, waiting, so far in vain, for his coming. But I am convinced that Jesus does not let a day pass without knocking on our door. Every day he comes to us, if only we are alert, if only we listen for his knock and open the door. He may come to us in the guise of a stranger, as a result of a chance encounter – as, in fact, he did to the man in the chariot, who should also be congratulated on his alertness and openness to the Gospel. If you or I had been in the chariot, perhaps we would have told Philip to go away, because we were trying to read our book. But the Ethiopian was alert, he heard Christ knocking at the door of his chariot, and he opened the door and let him in.

Let's take from the Gospel the command to stay awake and alert, not in the vague expectation of his coming, maybe in a thousand years, but in the certainty that he *will* come today, if we seize the opportunity either to receive him into our house, or, it may be, to introduce him to somebody else. A meeting with a sick or needy person is a meeting with Christ – Jesus tells us that what we did for them, we did for him. But also, in ministering to them, we are bringing Christ to them. Priests and other Eucharistic ministers do that in a very literal way, when they take Communion to the sick and housebound. But there are many ways to bring Christ to people. A sympathetic ear is the ear of Christ, a word of consolation is a word of Christ, a helping hand is the touch of Christ.

I have mentioned some obvious ways to encounter Christ, obvious because he has told us about them himself in the Gospel, and the Gospel passage is well known. But let us be alert to encounter Jesus in unexpected ways, in ways which are not spelt out in the Bible. The Son of Man is coming at an hour we do not expect, and no doubt in a way we do not expect, and in a guise we do not recognise. I don't know how you or I will encounter

Jesus today, in whose person or in what situation. But this I do know: he is there, today and every day, seeking an encounter with us, knocking at our door, passing by in his chariot, falling into conversation with us as we walk. And happy are we if we recognise him.

Twentieth Sunday of the Year
THE DEADLY PIT

Readings
Jer 38:4-6.8-10; Heb 12:1-4; Lk 12:49-53

People sometimes ask me why we read the Old Testament. Often its meaning is obscure and it seems to have very little relevance to our lives today. So why read it?

The short answer is, that if you don't understand the Old Testament, you haven't got a chance of understanding the New Testament. Jesus tells us, not once, but many times, that the Old Testament bears witness to him. He says to the Pharisees, 'You study the Scriptures, believing that in them you have eternal life; now these same Scriptures testify to me.' Again he says to them, 'If you really believed Moses you would believe me too, since it was I that he was writing about.'

When we look at the portions of Scripture he gives by way of example, we find that he had in mind not just one or two key passages, but all sorts of quotations from many different books. He cites the story of the brazen serpent from the Book of Numbers, the story of Jonah in the belly of the whale.

Furthermore, almost all his teaching derives from the Old Testament. He insists that he is not teaching them something new, but reminding them of what they should know already. He identifies as the first and greatest commandment a verse from the Book of Deuteronomy, to love the Lord God with all your heart and mind and strength; the second, to love your neighbour as yourself, is from the Book of Leviticus. Saint Matthew, and all the New Testament writers, saw in almost every detail of Jesus's life the fulfilment of some prophecy of the Old Testament. The titles by which we acclaim Jesus – the Messiah, the Christ, the Son of God, the Son of Man, the Son of David, the Saviour, the Redeemer – are all taken from the Old Testament, and we need to be familiar with it if we are to understand them.

Nor is the Old Testament always remote and obscure. The Book of Jeremiah, from which we read today, is one of the most accessible of the Old Testament books. Jeremiah was the most human character you could imagine, and it is very easy to sympathise with his plight. In his lifetime, the King of Babylon was besieging Jerusalem. The entire city was on a war footing, to resist him. God gave Jeremiah the most unpopular task of proclaiming that resistance was useless and was, in fact, contrary to God's will. The only hope of safety lay in surrender to the King of Babylon. Needless to say, Jeremiah became the most unpopular man in Jerusalem. The army leaders wanted him put to death, because he was sapping the morale of the soldiers. Though in the event he escaped death, he endured persecution and severe punishment. At one time he was thrown in a muddy pit, up to his neck. At times he breaks into the most heart-rending laments:

> The word of the Lord has meant for me insult, derision, all day long. I used to say, 'I will not think about him, I will not speak in his name any more.' Then there seemed to be a fire burning in my heart, imprisoned in my bones. the effort to restrain it wearied me, I could not bear it.

I find it very easy to identify with Jeremiah when I am called upon to do something unpopular; and, believe you me, every priest is called upon to be unpopular from time to time. I think too that our Lord must have been greatly impressed by the Book of Jeremiah, for it shows a man trying to do God's will however unpopular it made him and whatever suffering it entailed; and that was very much the mission of Jesus himself.

Our Psalm, too, speaks directly to us. We don't know who

wrote the psalms. They used to be attributed to King David, but probably they were written by many different people. It is tempting to think that today's psalm was written by Jeremiah, because it so exactly describes his situation:

I waited, I waited for the Lord, and he stooped down to me; he heard my cry. He drew me from the deadly pit, from the miry clay.

Jeremiah was, quite literally, pulled out of a deadly pit. We could, and do, apply the Psalm to Jesus, who died and was buried in a pit, but was raised up by God.

We can also apply the Psalm to our own personal situation. Often in our lives we find ourselves in a deadly pit: a pit of grief, a pit of despair, a pit of loneliness. It is beyond our own strength to climb out of that pit; we need to be pulled out by someone stronger than ourselves. We may very well want to make this psalm our own, especially those last lines, 'You are my rescuer, my help, O God, do not delay.' I imagine we could use those words in any trouble: in temptation, in danger, in anxiety, in debt, in sorrow. For ourselves, for our loved ones, for anyone we know in any difficulty or distress, we can pray that psalm: 'You are my rescuer, my help, O God, do not delay.'

Twenty-first Sunday of the Year
TRAINING

Readings
Isa 36:18-21; Heb 12:5-7.11-13; Lk 13:22-30

I was present once when a man of mature years was received into the Church. The priest, in his homily, spoke of the long process of formation which had brought him to this point: much prayer, much reading of the Bible, many conversations, many life-experiences.

The same could be said for any of us. Each one of us is engaged in a long process of training, of formation in the Christian life. This formation will be completed only in heaven, but we can, and are expected to, make a good beginning here and now in this life.

There are many aspects of our training which will be pleasant, a matter for rejoicing and thanksgiving. The joy of worshipping together, the privilege of receiving the sacraments, the pleasure of singing well-loved hymns or of reading favourite passages of the Scriptures, the excitement of a pilgrimage, the tranquillity of a retreat, the experience of the love of our families and of other members of the Christian community. All these are very positive, very uplifting, very edifying, and, hopefully, our religion contains a good ration of all of these.

But there are aspects of our training which are not so pleasant; as the Letter to the Hebrews tells us, suffering is part of our training. Suffering is not pleasant, but it is essential to our Christian formation. For example, the experience of illness is very unpleasant, but without it we would not realise our own weakness and so put our trust in God's mercy. Or think of the pain of bereavement, perhaps the greatest pain we are called upon to bear; but we have to learn to let people go to God and believe that he has a loving purpose for them. How else could we be prepared to let go of our own lives in death and return with equanimity to the God who made us? Or the pain of realising that we have done wrong, that we were not so perfect as we liked to believe, but need to say sorry to others and to God. This can be a most unpleasant thing to have to do; but if we never realise our own need of forgiveness, how can we learn to forgive others? And the ability to forgive is something we must learn at all costs. Before we can forgive we have first to suffer wrong. This is not a pleasant thing, but only after such experiences can we learn to forgive, and to make allowances for those who have wronged us, and to carry on loving them in spite of all. And only when we can do this can we claim to be like Christ, who suffered immense wrong and responded by saying, 'Father, forgive them, for they know not what they do.'

All these experiences can go badly wrong and have effects which are the opposite of beneficial. There are people who have lost their faith because they have suffered illness or bereavement. They say, 'If there were a God, how could he let such things happen?' There are people who have drifted away from the faith because of guilt. They have done something wrong and lack the courage, or the humility, to repent. There are people who have left the Church because of scandal. Somebody, perhaps a priest, has done something wrong and they have responded by saying, 'How dare these people call themselves Christians! I'm having nothing more to do with their Church.'

These responses are understandable; yet they are misguided, and amount simply to giving in to temptation. If we can accept the trials and tribulations of this life for what they are, God training us to be his sons and daughters, then they become real means of grace and they help us to grow in the Christian life. Someone who has learned to bear suffering and has discovered the need to ask forgiveness and knows how to forgive others, is a stronger and more Christ-like person for these things. As the Letter to the Hebrews says, Any punishment is most painful at the time, and far from pleasant; but later, in those on whom it has been used, it bears fruit in peace and goodness.

So hold up your limp arms and steady your trembling knees and smooth out the path you tread; then the injured limb will not be wrenched, it will grow strong again.

Twenty-second Sunday of the Year
THE PARABLE

Readings
Ecclus 3:17-20.28-29; Heb 12:18-19.22-24; Lk 14:1.7-14

Jesus went for a meal to the house of one of the leading Pharisees; and, says Saint Luke, while he was there, he told the guests a parable. Now what is a parable? A parable is a story, like that of the Prodigal Son or of the Good Samaritan, with a religious message. The trouble is, that Jesus doesn't tell them a story. He gives them a piece of straightforward instruction: When they go to a wedding feast, they are not to take the seats of honour, lest they be humbled, but rather, they are to take the lowest seat, from which their host will raise them up. That doesn't sound like a parable at all.

And yet it is. Luke rightly saw that Jesus was not concerned with good behaviour at a party. There are books of the Bible, which are full of the kind of advice a man might give his son about how to behave in public. The Book of Ecclesiasticus, which we have just read, says, 'My son, be gentle in carrying out your business, and you will be better loved than a lavish giver.' Good advice: but Jesus never concerns himself with such matters; or, shall we say, if this passage really is concerned with polite behaviour in public, then it is the only occasion on which Jesus gave utterance to what we might call worldly wisdom.

The teaching of Jesus is not wise, in the ordinary sense of the word. 'Blessed are the poor, blessed are the meek, blessed are those who mourn, blessed are you when people persecute you.' These are not counsels on how to make friends and influence people. Worldly wisdom teaches a person how to behave acceptably, how to fit into society. Anyone who follows the teaching of Jesus will stand out from society, will be the one who does not fit in. In this world, the poor are not blessed, the meek inherit nothing, those who hunger and thirst all too often go unsatisfied.

And so this teaching of Jesus really is a parable. He tells a sort of story about how people should behave at a wedding-feast, but it is really concerned with the heavenly wedding-feast, that is, the Kingdom of God. And standards in the Kingdom of God are very different from standards in the kingdom of this world. In the Kingdom of God, those who mourn here will be comforted, those who hunger and thirst will be satisfied, those who are poor will be enriched.

'Everyone who exalts himself, here in this world, will be

humbled in the Kingdom of God, and everyone who humbles himself here and now will be exalted in the Kingdom of God.' This is the most characteristic of all Jesus's teaching, and since Jesus always practises what he preaches, his whole ministry, his whole life, can be seen as a parable illustrating this teaching. Think of it: the Son of God, the Lord of the whole universe, is born as a man; and not even a great man, in a palace, but the poorest of men, born in a stable, living in an obscure village; an itinerant preacher, with no home of his own, no place to lay his head; accepting rejection, mockery, a humiliating death on a cross. Saint Paul summarises his life beautifully:

> He was in the form of God; yet he laid no claim to equality with God, but made himself nothing, assuming the form of a slave. Bearing the human likeness, sharing the human lot, he humbled himself, and was obedient, even to the point of death, death on a cross.

If that were the end, we might say that the life of Jesus was a wonderful example, but an example to be admired rather than imitated, for who would wish to imitate an example which ended inevitably in rejection, humiliation and death?

But death on a cross is not the end; the resurrection opens for us the way to the Kingdom which belongs to the poor in spirit, where those who mourn shall be comforted and the merciful shall obtain mercy, where those who have taken the lowest seat will be called up higher, like Jesus himself, who took the lowliest place in death, for which reason, says Saint Paul,

> God has highly exalted him and bestowed on him the name which is above every name, that at the name of Jesus every knee should bow, in heaven and on earth and under the earth, and every tongue confess that Jesus Christ is Lord, to the glory of God the Father.

Twenty-third Sunday of the Year
COUNTING THE COST

Readings
Wis 9:13-18; Philemon 9-10.12-17; Lk 14:25-33

Our Lord tells us very clearly that before we become disciples, we must sit down and count the cost. It's no good starting something we can't finish – as Jesus puts it, starting to build a tower which we haven't the money to complete, or getting into a war which we haven't the resources to prosecute. To be a disciple of Jesus takes more than a rosy glow of benevolence. It takes resources of courage, of patience, of generosity of spirit.

Actually it takes more than we have, and we ask God himself to give us the grace, the courage, the generosity, to follow Jesus. But to make room for these resources we have to clear out a lot of unwanted lumber. We may need to renounce some inappropriate attitudes. Paul writes to Philemon on behalf of the slave Onesimus. Both men had become Christians, and now it was inappropriate for Philemon to continue to regard Onesimus as his slave. The clear implication of Paul's letter is that Philemon should set Onesimus free. That would be a considerable renunciation; a slave, in those days, was a very valuable commodity. But of what use would it be for Philemon to pray for grace, for generosity, for forgiveness of his sins, while keeping a fellow-Christian in bondage as a slave?

To be disciples of Jesus, there will be things we need to renounce. Like Philemon, we may need to renounce the smug satisfaction of regarding others as our inferiors, as our slaves, put on earth solely to do our bidding.

But there will also be things which we should on no account renounce. Despite our Lord's words, I do not think we should renounce our mothers and fathers, our wives and husbands, our children, or our brothers and sisters. There are some who have made themselves and their families very unhappy by a literal obedience to those words. Our families may in fact compose part of the cross Jesus calls us to bear. Difficult and unhappy relationships cannot always be renounced; they must sometimes be borne. An unreasonable parent, an unsympathetic husband, an ungrateful and wayward child, may perhaps be not a distraction from following Christ, but the very way in which we do follow him.

It may be, at the last judgement, that Jesus will say to us, 'Come into the kingdom prepared for the saints! For when I was sick you visited me, when I was hungry you fed me, when I was troubled you comforted me.' And we shall say, 'But Lord, when you were sick I didn't visit you; I was too busy visiting my sick mother. And when you were hungry I didn't feed you; I was too busy feeding my children. And when you were troubled I didn't comfort you; I was too busy comforting my wretched husband.' And Jesus will say, 'Yes, and in ministering to them, the least of my brothers and sisters, you were ministering to me.'

Twenty-fourth Sunday of the Year
GRACE ABOUNDING

Readings
Ex 32:7-11.13-14; 1 Tim 1:12-17; Lk 15:1-32

Our readings seem to offer a number of stories all about repentance: 'There will be more rejoicing in heaven over one repentant sinner than over ninety-nine virtuous men who have no need of repentance.' If we look a little closer, though, we see that the stories are not about repentance at all, but about something rather different.

The Israelites had abandoned their God. They had made themselves an idol in the shape of a golden calf and were giving it credit for bringing them out of Egypt: an act of apostasy remarkable both for its ingratitude and its stupidity. God proposes to destroy them, or, as he puts it, 'My wrath shall blaze out against them and devour them.' Moses pleads for them, and God relents, and does not bring on his people the disaster he had threatened.

But this was not because they had repented. In point of fact they had not repented. Even as God was speaking to Moses, they were still worshipping their idol. God forgave them, not because they had repented, but freely, for no other reason except that he chose to.

And this is what we mean by grace. Grace is God's free gift, given to people who have done nothing to deserve it, solely because God loves them. Paul writes to that effect to the Ephesians:

It is by God's grace that you have been saved, through faith. It is not your own doing, but God's gift. There is nothing here to boast of, since it is not the result of your own efforts.

We find the same thing in Saint Paul's letter to Timothy. Paul writes,

I thank Christ Jesus our Lord, who has given me strength, and who judged me faithful enough to call me into his service even though I used to be a blasphemer and did all I could to injure and discredit the faith.

Paul had been active in persecuting the Christians; in fact he was on the way to Damascus to have some of them put to death, when Christ met him on the road. We would not have been surprised if God had met Paul on the road and killed him, but that's not what God did. He chose to make Paul an example of abundant grace given to sinners, of whom Paul acknowledged himself to be the worst. As Paul himself says, 'The grace of our Lord filled me with faith and with the love that is in Christ Jesus.'

In the Gospel we are given three stories, apparently about repentance. A sheep goes missing. The good shepherd leaves the other ninety-nine in the wilderness and goes after it, and finds it, and brings it home. Now this is not a story about repentance. The sheep does not repent. It does not return to the flock of its own accord. It continues to wander further and further away. The point of the story is the effort the good shepherd makes to retrieve it. Again, the story is an example of the grace of God, who seeks out and finds those who stray from his paths, not because they deserve it, but because he loves them.

Or again, a woman loses a coin. The story is not about the coin making its own way back into her purse; that it cannot do. The story concerns the woman's extraordinary efforts to find that lost coin. She lights a lamp, she sweeps the room thoroughly. The woman represents God. What does 'to light a lamp' mean, if not to send into the world our Lord Jesus Christ, the Light of the World? And the sending of Christ into the world is God's great act of grace.

Our last story is different. The Prodigal Son does, after all, repent: 'I will leave this place and go to my father and say, Father, I have sinned against heaven and against you.' Yes, there is a measure of repentance there; but how much more emphasis there is on the actions of the father. While the son is still a long way off – not only physically, but in terms of the quality of his repentance; in this area too he still has a long way to go – while he is still a long way off, the father runs to him, clasps him in his arms and kisses him, and receives him back with joy and festivity. The quality of the forgiveness is very different from the quality of the repentance, and again is an image of God's overflowing grace.

Have you experienced that overflowing grace in your own life? Has God shown you mercy when you know that you did not deserve it? Then welcome to the Church, and indeed to the whole human race, because that is how God treats all his children. So much did he love us that he sent his only Son to die for us. As Saint Paul says, once again, 'What proves that God loves us is that Christ died for us while we were still sinners.' Which is what we mean by grace.

Twenty-fifth Sunday of the Year
AMOS

Readings
Amos 8:4-7; 1 Tim 2:1-8; Lk 16:1-13

I don't know if the justice and peace movement has a patron saint; but if they ever advertise for the job, the prophet Amos will be in with a chance, because he is, above all, the prophet of social justice. Other prophets had their particular message and ministry. We think of Isaiah as pre-eminently the prophet of the Messiah. Although the book of Isaiah was written by several different people, at several different times, all of them look forward to a messianic kingdom of righteousness. Jeremiah was perhaps the most courageous of the prophets, called to proclaim an unpopular and dangerous message and suffering persecution for it. Hosea was told to take an adulterous woman in marriage, as an image of Israel's infidelity to God and God's love for Israel in spite of that. And each of the prophets was called to proclaim some particular message, given especially to him. Perhaps Isaiah couldn't have proclaimed Jeremiah's message, or maybe Amos couldn't have spoken as Hosea did.

The special message of Amos is set out clearly in the opening words of our reading: 'Listen to this, you who trample on the needy, and try to suppress the poor people of the country.' His message is one of justice, of fair dealing with the poor. He complains of people who cannot wait for the religious festivals to be over, so that they can pursue their real interest – making money. Their religion is for them just a tiresome interruption of real life. There are Christians for whom religion is something you do on Sundays, in church, and which has no relevance to the way they lead their lives during the rest of the week. The people whom Amos denounces are merchants who use dishonest weights and measures in order to swindle their customers, even if those customers are desperately poor. For these people, religion is religion, and business is business, and they see no connection between the two.

Amos lived in the eighth century B.C. His career as a prophet took place between about 760 and 750 B.C. And that makes him the earliest of the prophets. There had been prophets before Amos, but they tended to be what we would call fortune-tellers, telling the kings whether they would have success or otherwise in war, advising them whether or not it was an auspicious day to fight a battle. They were professionals. There were guilds of such people, known as the Sons of the Prophets.

Amos bore no relation to such people. When he was challenged, he said that he was not a prophet, nor one of the Sons of the Prophets, but he was a herdsman and a dresser of sycamore trees. In other words, he was a perfectly ordinary chap, a working man with no religious functions. And God called him to deliver his message.

This raises two considerations in my mind. The first is, that Amos, the first of the Old Testament prophets, has a message of social justice. That message has been at the forefront of the Church's teaching in recent years. Some people might ask if this is something new, something perhaps peripheral to the Gospel of salvation, some fashionable trend which the Church has taken up in recent years. It isn't: the story of Amos teaches us that the very first time God sent someone with a message to the people of Israel, it was a message of justice and fair dealing.

The second consideration is, that Amos was an ordinary chap, just like you and me, and he was called to perform a very extraordinary mission. To what extraordinary mission is he calling you and me? Depend upon it, God has work for us, work that nobody else can do for us.

Twenty-sixth Sunday of the Year
DIVES AND LAZARUS

Readings
Amos 6:1.4-7; 1 Tim 6:11-16; Lk 16:19-31

What do you miss most about the good old days? Is it the long, hot summers? Is it the possibility of going out leaving your door unlocked? Is it the community spirit? Or is it, perhaps, the hell-fire sermons? People ask me, 'Whatever happened to Hell? We used to have lovely sermons about it in the old days.'

Well, Luke tells us a story about a man who goes to Hell. And pretty unpleasant it is. He lies in torment and agony in the fires of Hell. What does he do to merit such a terrible punishment? All the Gospel says is that he is rich, and used to dress in purple and fine linen and feast magnificently every day. A bit over the top, but is it such a crime to be rich? There must have been many rich people around in Jesus's day. Did they all go to Hell? What was so especially bad about this man's style of richness?

He had a poor man, Lazarus, on his doorstep. Literally on his doorstep: he passed him every time he went in and out. Lazarus was starving, and would have longed to eat the scraps that fell from the rich man's table; but the rich man never gave him any. Lazarus was covered in sores, but the rich man never did anything to relieve his pain. Lazarus was naked, and the rich man was dressed in purple and fine linen, but he never gave Lazarus a shirt to cover his sores and stop the dogs from licking them.

Other people might be rich, but perhaps they did something for those less fortunate than themselves. Or perhaps they could plead, 'We never knew, we never realised, that there was such suffering. If only we had known, we would have done something for that poor wretch. Perhaps we were thoughtless, but we weren't deliberately cruel.' The rich man in our parable could offer no such excuse: Lazarus was *there*, right on his doorstep. Every day he saw his suffering, and he did nothing to help. He shared nothing with Lazarus, he did nothing to acknowledge their common humanity.

There was a time when perhaps, the people of our own country knew nothing about the great suffering in the world. From the beginning of time there have been famines in Africa and floods in Bangladesh. But *we* didn't know about them. Television has brought the whole world to our doorstep. And I think that in one respect, television has made a great contribution to the progress of the Kingdom of God. It is evident to everyone nowadays, there is no escaping the fact, that all people are our brothers and sisters. The lawyer asked Jesus, 'Who is my neighbour?' Thanks to television, people in Africa and Asia, in South America and the Philippines, are all our neighbours. We know very well what are their problems and their needs.

And that puts us all in the position of the rich man in the parable. We cannot plead ignorance. These people are on our doorstep. So we must ask ourselves rather different questions from the ones we asked when we *were* ignorant. Many manuals of devotion have a list of questions we should ask ourselves when preparing to make a confession, or indeed to receive Communion. I find for example in my Sunday Missal, 'Am I just, conscientious, honest, in my work? Do I tell the truth? Have I stolen what is not mine?' These are perfectly good questions, and we are right to ask them.

But I think in today's world we must ask ourselves a few more questions, like perhaps: 'Have I stolen from the poor by buying unfairly traded goods? Have I denied the poor justice by failing to campaign for the reduction of their debt? Have I harboured uncharitable attitudes by suggesting that the poor are the author of their own misfortunes, by having too many children or living in the wrong place?' All of which, in today's world, are really equivalent to asking, 'Have I ignored Lazarus on my doorstep?'

Twenty-seventh Sunday of the Year
MUSTARD SEED

Readings
Hab 1:2-3; 2:2-4; 2 Tim 1:6-8.13-14; Lk 17:5-10

What a tiny thing a virus is! It is so small that you need a high-powered microscope to see it. But what a lot of harm it can do. Our foot-and-mouth epidemic started, no doubt, with one sheep on one farm being infected by a tiny virus. What great consequences can come from tiny beginnings! Or again, one tiny cigarette butt, carelessly thrown away, can start a forest fire that lays bare hundreds of square miles of woodland.

Perhaps Saint Paul had such an image in mind when he urged Timothy to fan into a flame the gift that had been given to him at his ordination. The original apostles, you will recall, had tongues of flame descend on them at Pentecost. Neither Paul nor Timothy had been members of that original group, but each had subsequently received the flame of the Holy Spirit. Saint Paul had used his flame to set fire to most of the ancient world. It is astonishing to read of his travels in the New Testament, how he set Galatia and Philippi, Ephesus and Thessalonica, Corinth, Colossae, and Rome itself, on fire with the Good News of Jesus Christ. Can so much have been done by one man, and by a man who began as an enemy of the Christian faith?

Jesus gives us another image, that of the mustard seed. Were our faith only the size of a mustard seed, we could perform great miracles. A mustard seed may be tiny, but it grows into a great shrub. In the place where I often take my holidays, there is a great vine which gives shade not only to one restaurant, but to a whole street of restaurants. Hundreds of people take their meals under its canopy. And yet it is only one vine, and it grew from a single grape seed.

When I reflect on the mustard seed I cannot be despondent. There is much talk nowadays about the Church shrinking in size, about it not producing enough priests, about parishes having to be amalgamated. I don't think we have sufficient confidence in the Church's ability to grow, as a vine does from a grape seed, or as a great fire grows from a single spark. Perhaps one of us here will fan that spark into such a flame as will consume the world.

Why should it not be one of us? Saint Francis, whose day we celebrate about now, was a very ordinary young man. And yet the fire took such a hold in him that he founded a movement which changed the world. Ignatius Loyola read of the deeds of Francis, and thought, 'What if I should do as Francis did, or as Dominic did?' And Ignatius founded another movement which took the Gospel to Japan and China. Who is there here who will fan the flame into such a conflagration as will make us forget about a shortage of priests, or a shortage of anything else?

God is not short of resources to make his Church grow. He can bring the great vine out of the grape seed, the great blaze out of the tiny spark. It takes only one of us to fan the spark into a flame. Who will it be? Whom shall we send? Is it I Lord? Is it you?

Twenty-eighth Sunday of the Year
STRANGERS

Readings
2 Kgs 5:14-17; 2 Tim 2:8-13; Lk 17:11-19

If you read the history of the Old Testament, you will find that the Syrians were no friends to the people of Israel. As often as not, they were at war with them. But when Naaman, the Syrian, is afflicted with leprosy he seeks help from the God of Israel, and finds it. Evidently God does not restrict his healing love to his chosen people; it is poured out also upon their neighbours, even their enemies. Again, in the Gospel one of the lepers is a Samaritan, a member of a people at odds with the Jews. He is not for that reason denied healing.

We, as Christians and Catholics, have to beware of supposing that we have a monopoly of God's love. God loves all his children, all those who were created in his image, and wants to give them all his love, his healing, his peace; he loves them whatever their race, whatever their religion, whether or not they obey his laws, whether or not they are afterwards thankful for his kindness.

If God loves everybody, and cares for everybody, and wants to heal everybody, why be a Christian? Would we not be just as well off in some other religion, or as complete heathens? Would he not love us just as much? If our only concern with God is what we can get out of him, then that argument may hold water. But if that really is our attitude, then we are very ungrateful children of God, like those nine lepers who couldn't be bothered to thank God for their cure. Hopefully, we are not like that. We want to love God, because he first loved us. We know what a tremendous privilege it is that he has called us his children, and we want to live as his children.

How do we live as his children? Saint Paul gives us some hints. If we have died with him, then we shall live with him. We die with him, in the first place, at our Baptism. But Paul is not concerned solely with the rite of Baptism. We need to die, not once but every day, by putting to death those things in us which are unworthy of him: anger, selfishness, pride, greed. Whenever they raise their head, we need to swat them as we would swat a fly. It's painful, because unlike a fly they are inside us, they are part of us.

But above all, we show ourselves to be children of God when we show gratitude for his goodness. The Samaritan turned back to give thanks, and in doing so he showed himself more truly a child of God than those who could claim the title by birth. Thanksgiving: the very name of our principal service, the Eucharist, means thanksgiving. But, just as we would be poor Christians if the only time we died to self was at our Baptism, so we should be very poor Christians indeed if the only time we showed thankfulness to God was at Mass. 'Thank you' should be the words most often on our lips from the beginning of the day to its end.

We might begin the day by praying: 'Thank you, Lord, for this new day. Thank you for my parents, my children, my wife, my husband, for all my loved ones. Thank you for the food I eat, for the air I breathe. Thank you for my work, for my friends, for my education. Thank you for my worldly goods, thank you for the hope of heaven. Thank you for my health, thank you for forgiving me my sins, thank you for calling me your child. Thank you for sending your Son to die for me. Thank you for the Mass, thank you for speaking to me in the Scriptures, thank you for allowing me to speak to you in my prayers. Thank you for all your gifts, thank you for all that is good.'

Is there anything in all God's creation for which we should not thank our God?

Twenty-ninth Sunday of the Year
NEVER GIVE UP

Readings
Ex 17:8-13; 2 Tim 3:14–4:2; Lk 18:1-8

There's a little book I'm rather fond of, called *The Way of a Pilgrim*, written by an anonymous Russian in the last century.

The Pilgrim has heard a text from the letters of Saint Paul, 'Pray without ceasing,' and he is anxious to find out how this can be done. He asks various people, but they are unable to give him the answer. At last he finds an old monk who does know how it's done. The monk teaches the Pilgrim a certain prayer, and tells him to go away and recite it three thousand times a day. The Pilgrim goes away for a week or two, then returns and tells his director that he can now recite the prayer three thousand times a day without difficulty. The monk tells him to recite it six thousand times a day. Again, the Pilgrim goes away, and returns when he has mastered this feat. His director now tells him to recite it twelve thousand times a day. And when he can do that, the Pilgrim is allowed to recite the prayer as often as he wishes, day and night, without ceasing.

All of which may seem a bit over the top. We have so much to do in our lives: to hold down a job, or it may be, to keep house, to care for a family, to study. There are very few people, even contemplative monks and nuns, who have nothing else to do in their lives but pray. And yet the Bible teaches us again and again that prayer is the first essential, that the fact that we have other calls on our time is no excuse not to pray. We find indeed that all those other things we have to do come to nothing if they are not preceded, supported and surrounded by prayer.

The Old Testament story gives the example of Moses keeping his hands raised in prayer while Israel battles with the Amalekites. As long as he persists in prayer, Israel has the upper hand, but when he tires and his arms fall to his side, the Amalekites gain the advantage. We need not be so dull as to see only the literal meaning. Clearly, whatever battles we undertake, whether literal or moral or spiritual, whether we battle against temptation or injustice or prejudice or indifference, our efforts will achieve nothing unless they are accompanied by fervent and continuous prayer.

Our Lord teaches the same thing in the Gospel. A widow pleads for justice to an unjust judge. He cares nothing for the woman's plight, but her persistence so wears him out that eventually he grants her request.

This is not some unusual or uncharacteristic feature of our Lord's teaching: he says the same thing again, in another parable. A man comes to the door at midnight and asks for some bread. The man inside is in bed and has no interest whatever in getting up and supplying his neighbour's needs, but the continual knocking on the door forces him to do so. Or again, as Jesus enters Jericho, a blind beggar calls out, 'Jesus, Son of David, have pity on me.' Those around him tell him to be quiet, but he does not keep quiet, he calls out all the louder, 'Son of David, have pity on me.' And the Son of David does take pity on him, and restores his sight: an object lesson to us all in persistence in prayer. Again, a Syro-Phoenician woman begs him to cure her daughter. Jesus, no doubt to test her faith, refuses her request, in fact, is quite rude to her. But she will not take no for an answer, and her daughter is cured.

What is the hardest thing to do in the world? Climb Mount Everest? Run a marathon? Learn Chinese? No, the hardest thing in the world is to bring up a family, to keep it together, to teach our children decent values. It's almost impossible, there are so many difficulties, so many heartbreaks and disappointments. Nobody can achieve such a task without the aid of constant prayer. When we hear Jesus, or Saint Paul teaching us to pray without ceasing, we may think, 'That's all right for nuns, but Jesus and Paul didn't have to bring up a family.' Actually, it's precisely to ordinary people, to people with jobs to hold down and families to hold together, that Jesus and Paul are speaking. We should pray without ceasing: because we have the hardest job on earth, and without prayer we shall never succeed.

Thirtieth Sunday of the Year
THE PHARISEE IN THE TEMPLE

Readings
Ecclesus 35:12-14.16-19; 2 Tim 4:6-8.16-18; Lk 18:9-14

I once saw a film called *The Devil's Advocate*. I don't know that I would particularly recommend it; there was a lot in it that was fantastic or even silly, but there were also things in it that are thought-provoking.

The story concerns a young lawyer who has never lost a case. The film opens with him procuring the acquittal of a child-molester. He is taken on by a big law firm whose boss turns out to be Satan, played ably by Al Pacino. The young lawyer does very well for his masters, using his considerable skill to pervert the course of justice, and in the process neglecting his wife to such an extent that she eventually commits suicide. Only then does he realise how his obsession with being the best at his job is truly Satanic. As can only happen in films, he is given a second chance. The film returns to the point where he was defending the child-molester. He causes a sensation by refusing to continue with the case.

He may seem to have found salvation, but even now the devil is waiting in the wings: there is a hint at the end that his new determination to be the most honest lawyer ever rather than the most successful, may be just as much the product of pride as his former ambition, and in the end just as destructive. Whatever we do, however praiseworthy, its value is reduced or destroyed if we take on board this diabolical pride in being better than everybody else at it.

If you have ever watched the series *Father Ted*, you will know that it was Father Ted's ambition to win the Golden Cleric award. I most sincerely hope that they never do introduce a Golden Cleric award, because if they do there'll be no possibility of salvation for the clergy. A priest whose pride would not let him lose a soul would be in danger of losing his own. I mean no offence to the many admirable people who earn their living as professional athletes, but, speaking only for myself, I would be worried about being in a profession which of its nature involved being faster or stronger than everybody else. I would be worried about losing the one race which really matters, the race of which Saint Paul says, 'I have run the race to the finish.'

We see in our Gospel a man who has many admirable qualities: he is not grasping, or unjust. He fasts twice a week and pays his tithes. So far so good. But he has to be better at being good than everybody else, better than the wretched tax-collector beside him. He's a pretty egregious example of the sin of pride. No doubt, we could make a better fist of being humble than he did. But let's not be too confident that we are better than he is; otherwise we may find ourselves saying, 'I thank you, God, that I am not proud, vain, conceited like the rest of mankind, and particularly that I am not like this Pharisee here.' The Devil would like nothing better than to find us proud of our humility.

Thirty-first Sunday of the Year
ZACCHAEUS

Readings
Wis 11:22–12:2; 2 Thess 1:11–2:2; Lk 19:1-10

What was it that motivated Zacchaeus to want to see Jesus? Was it simple curiosity? After all, Jesus was building up a reputation as a healer and a teacher. He had become a celebrity. No doubt if a famous actor or musician, or a member of the royal family, were to come to our town, we would want to see that person, simply because that person was famous. But you can't go to see Jesus as you would go to see Prince Charles, or your favourite film star. Those people may acknowledge your applause, or wave back to you, but they do not turn on you and demand that you give up your lives to follow them. You take a risk when you become curious about Jeus.

Perhaps, though, it was more than curiosity which drove Zacchaeus up that tree. Perhaps Zacchaeus was attracted to Jesus in the way that opposites attract each other. Jesus was a holy man, and Zacchaeus was anything but a holy man. Jesus possessed the qualities that Zacchaeus conspicuously lacked. Perhaps Zacchaeus was consciously seeking to fill a void in his life.

Whatever drew Zacchaeus to Jesus, it brought about his salvation. Jesus invited himself into Zaccheus's life, and Zacchaeus was never the same again.

What is it that attracts *us* to Jesus? Sometimes I feel that I hardly know him. His words and actions are a constant surprise to me, even though I have studied them for years. The Gospels tell us so little about him. And yet, I have given up most of my life to following him, and proclaiming him, and persuading others to follow him.

I don't always feel that my discipleship is entirely voluntary. Sometimes I feel like the prophet Jeremiah, who said, 'I used to say, I will not think about him, I will not speak in his name any more. Then there seemed to be a fire burning in my heart, imprisoned in my bones. The effort to restrain it wearied me, I could not bear it.'

Or again I think of the words of Saint Paul: 'I do not boast of preaching the gospel, since it is a duty which has been laid on me; I should be punished if I did *not* preach it!'

But enough about me. What is it that attracts *you* to Jesus? Why have you come, like Zacchaeus, to catch a glimpse of him? Because that is exactly what you do at Mass. You hear his words, you come close to him in the sacrament. What are you looking for?

For meaning and purpose in your life? So often life seems devoid of meaning. Often we wonder what it's all in aid of. Jesus assures us that life has a purpose, and he is that purpose. He is, as he put it, the way, the truth and the life. The way back to God the Father, who created us and put us here, the truth about life, the life itself.

Or are you looking for forgiveness? Zacchaeus needed desperately to be forgiven for his many crimes, and he found that forgiveness in Jesus. Jesus stands ready to forgive us our sins; he died on the cross precisely to do that.

Are you looking for the assurance that you matter, that you are not just an insignificant event in a vast universe? Jesus gave Zacchaeus just such assurance, and he offers it to us. We matter: he died for us, and loves us still.

Are you afraid of dying, and looking for some hope that death is not the end, that you will not simply be snuffed out like a spent candle? Jesus rose from the dead, and showed us the truth of the resurrection. He has the message of eternal life.

Thirty-second Sunday of the Year
MACCABEES

Readings
2 Macc 7:1.9-14 2 Thess 2:16–3:5; Lk 20:27-38

You could be forgiven if you'd never heard of the Second Book of the Maccabees; or indeed of the First Book of the Maccabees. These are not among the best-known books of the Bible. Part of the reason that we are being offered a reading from this book is that we are almost at the end of our three-year cycle. In a couple of weeks' time we shall start reading the Bible all over again. In the course of three years we read most of the Bible at the Sunday Mass, and by the end of the three years we're rather scraping the barrel for interesting readings.

But the books of the Maccabees are not simply the bits of the Bible left over when we've read all the interesting bits. They have a genuine interest all of their own. They are part of a group of books written about 160 years before the birth of Christ. The best known member of this group is the Book of Daniel, which covers the same subject-matter as the Maccabees, though in a very different way.

The historical event which gave rise to these books was the Great Persecution, which began in the year 167 BC. At that time the Jews were ruled by a king called Antiochus Epiphanes. He was a Greek, and tried to impose Greek culture and religion on the Jews. He desecrated the Jewish temple and forced the Jews to offer sacrifice to his Greek gods. Those who refused were put to death.

A revolt was led by one Judas Maccabeus; whence the name, the Book of Maccabees. Judas Maccabeus defeated the Greek tyrant and restored the worship in the temple in Jerusalem. The re-consecration of the temple is celebrated to this day by the Jews at the feast of Hannukah, which falls about the time of our Christmas. The Books of Maccabees tell of the events of this period in a factual way.

The Book of Daniel, on the other hand, chose to tell the story of an ancient hero called Daniel, who is said to have lived at the time of the exile in Babylon. In that book, three young men refuse to worship the Babylonian gods and are thrown into a burning fiery furnace. Daniel himself insists on worshipping the God of the Jews, and is thrown into a lions' den. All are saved from death by an angel.

The message was clear for those living at the time of the Great Persecution. All this had happened before. The King of Babylon had tried to force the Jews to abandon their religion, and he had come to a sticky end. The Jews who had remained faithful to their religion, however, had been delivered from their afflictions. Likewise, King Antiochus Epiphanes would come to a sticky end, and those Jews who remained faithful would be preserved. The Jewish people must therefore trust in God and remain faithful: the persecution would last only a short time.

We find also in these books a new belief creeping into the Jewish religion: the hope of the resurrection. Unlike many religions, the Jewish religion had no belief in, and no interest in, an afterlife. This is quite a remarkable thing. The Egyptians believed in an afterlife, which is why they took such care to mummify the bodies of those who died, and to bury them in elaborate tombs. And most of the people of the ancient world believed in some kind of afterlife. Not so the Hebrews: when you were dead, you were dead, and that was that. It is only in the period of the Maccabees that at least some of them began to believe in a resurrection after death. That is why the second brother in our story exclaimed, 'Inhuman fiend, you may discharge us from this present life, but the King of the world will raise us up.' He was expressing a new and revolutionary belief. His brothers say much the same thing. The fourth brother says he is 'relying on God's promise that we shall be raised up by him, whereas for you there can be no resurrection, no new life.'

By the time of Jesus, the Jews were split on the question of the resurrection. The two factions with differing views in the matter were called the Pharisees and the Sadducees. We usually think of the Pharisees as the opponents of Jesus, but in this matter they saw eye to eye with him. They believed in the resurrection. The Sadducees, on the other hand, were what we would call a fundamentalist sect. They accepted only the oldest books of the Bible, the first five books, traditionally attributed to Moses. Here there is no mention of a resurrection, and therefore they rejected the resurrection as a novelty imported into their religion.

That is why they asked Jesus the rather silly question about the widow who married seven times, intending to poke fun at the idea of the resurrection. Jesus replies to them with a saying of great profundity. He refers to the Book of Exodus, one of the few books which the Sadducees did accept. God is content to be called the God of Abraham, the God of Isaac and God of Jacob. He is God, not of the dead, but of the living; for to him all men are in fact alive. The God of infinite power and love is not going to create someone he loves and after whom he is content to be named, and then simply let that person cease to exist.

Are we to suppose that God continually suffers bereavement, losing people that he loves but has no power to preserve? Surely not! Surely he will raise them eternal, as he himself is eternal. An interesting and beautiful thought; and Jesus proves the truth of that thought, when he rises triumphant from the grave, and shows Thomas the holes in his hands and in his feet, the living proof of the resurrection.

Thirty-third Sunday of the Year
THE END

Readings
Mal 3:19-20; 2 Thess 3:7-12; Lk 21:5-19

What if the universe should come to an end? I know that I myself will come to an end, one day. I have done too many funerals to indulge in the fantasy that I shall live for ever. But I tell myself, that even if I come to an end, the world will go on.

And perhaps I shall have made a difference to the world. Perhaps people will look back at something I said, or something I wrote, and say that it made a lasting change to the way people think or feel. Shakespeare lives on in his plays, Beethoven lives on in his symphonies, Michaelangelo lives on in his paintings and in his sculptures. Could I not live on in my sermons?

Perhaps so, as long as there were people to read them. But what if there were no more people? What if the human race itself had come to an end? What if this world, and every one of the millions of worlds created by God, had come to an end, and there was no one left to know that they had ever existed?

An alarming thought; and yet, the universe *will* one day come to an end. Our Scriptures talk about nothing so much as the end of things. Malachi talks of the wicked coming to an end, and a rather sticky end at that. Our Lord talks in the Gospel about the Temple, and the holy city of Jerusalem, coming to an end. In the Book of Revelation, Saint John describes how the earth and the sky vanished, leaving no trace.

All this would be very depressing, if that little word 'end' did not have another meaning. Something comes to an end when it ceases to exist. But to what end did it come into being in the first place? To what end did God make us? That is, for what purpose? Our faith teaches us that God made us, to the end that we might know him, and love him, and share eternal life with him. Eternal life is our true end; and though this mortal body should perish, and though this earth should crumble to dust, and though the very dust should evaporate into nothingness, God's love endures and will endure, and we shall endure, for we are the object of his love.

God will let nothing which he loves, perish. We are assured of that again and again. In the Book of Wisdom we read, 'Death was never of God's fashioning; not for his pleasure does life cease to be; what meant his creation, but that all created things should have being?' And Jesus himself says, 'I am the resurrection. If anyone believes in me, even though he dies he will live, and whoever lives and believes in me will never die.' Saint Augustine, at the end of his book, *The City of God*, talks about our end, as we enjoy for ever the vision of God for which we were created:

> There we shall rest and we shall see, we shall see and we shall love, we shall love and we shall praise. For what other end do we propose to ourselves than to attain to the kingdom of which there is no end?

Thirty-fourth Sunday of the Year
CHRIST THE KING

Readings
2 Sam 5:1-3; Col 1:12-20; Lk 23:35-43

'The people stayed there before the cross watching Jesus.' And what a pitiful sight he must have looked: his body torn and twisted, lacerated by the scourge and pierced by the nails, his face bloody from the crown of thorns. It would be hard to imagine anyone looking less like a king. And yet that is how our crucifix portrays him, looking beneath the surface blood and sweat at the majesty concealed beneath.

That too is how Saint Luke sees him, for amid all the suffering he has him perform a truly royal action. 'I promise you,' Jesus says to the penitent thief, 'Today you will be with me in paradise.' He offers a royal pardon to that thief. And not only to the thief; on behalf of those who are crucifying him he pleads, 'Father, forgive them, for they know not what they do.'

Those standing near the cross see nothing of his majesty. They jeer at him, says Saint Luke, they mock him, they abuse him. They see only what is on the surface. They have no eyes to pierce beneath the surface to see the God in hiding.

How sharp are our own eyes? Can we see beneath the surface of things, beneath the surface of people? Our eyes light upon some poor beggar, or perhaps some sick person, disfigured by poverty, by age, by illness. Do we see an unattractive, even repulsive object? Or can we perceive Christ in that person?

It is very necessary to sharpen our spiritual vision, for our religion is all about perceiving what is below the surface and is therefore not obvious. I hold up a piece of bread. To our bodily eyes, it is just that, a piece of bread; but to the eyes of the spirit it is the Body of Christ. A beggar squats beside the roadside. To our bodily eyes, he is no more than a degraded wretch; to the eyes of the Spirit he is a man made in God's image, redeemed by Christ who does indeed dwell within him. A man hangs bloody and torn upon the cross. To our bodily eyes, he is a criminal, executed by process of law; to the eyes of the spirit he is the king of heaven and earth, the image of the unseen God.

How much more rich and wonderful, how much more truly God's creation, is the world, if we can look at it with the eyes of the spirit rather than with the eyes of the body. How much more wonderful are we ourselves, if we can look into ourselves with the eyes of the spirit.

We do sometimes look deeply into ourselves, to examine our consciences, and we see there the nasty and unworthy things we have done. I wouldn't want to discourage anyone from making an examination of conscience; in fact, we ought to do it more often. But surely we ought to look also into the wonder of our being, that being created by God in his own image, redeemed by the blood of Christ and destined for eternal life with him.

The Psalmist was accustomed to look into himself with the eyes of the spirit. He says in one psalm, 'It was you who created my being, knit me together in my mother's womb. I thank you for the wonder of my being, for the wonders of all your creation.'

We should do well to enlarge the eyes of our spirit, and ponder more on the wonders of God's creation. But how can we do this? The way to enlarge our faculties is by exercising them. So let's exercise our spiritual eye. Let's think of any person: preferably not a grand or important person, but somebody quite humble. Better still, let it be somebody we dislike, or at least find it hard to get on with. Now let us consider the wonders of that person's being; reflect that the person in question is a mighty work of God, created in God's image, loved by God, redeemed by the blood of Christ; that Christ himself dwells in that person. Already, I think, the eyes of our spirit are being opened.

Can we perform the same exercise on all the people we meet? Can we reflect that the person we meet in the street, in the shop, at work, at school, in church, is a palace in which dwells Christ our King? And do we consider that it's no use honouring Christ or King, enthroned upon the altar, if we don't honour Christ our King, enthroned in the least of his brothers?

For information about our magazines

> *Doctrine & Life* (ten times a year)
>
> *Religious Life Review* (six times a year)
>
> SCRIPTURE IN CHURCH (four times a year)
>
> *Spirituality* (six times a year)

and about our range of books on

> preaching
>
> liturgy
>
> Church documents
>
> religious life
>
> spirituality
>
> current questions

visit our website

www.DominicanPublications.com

All by Bill East and published by Dominican Publications

www.DominicanPublications.com

Follow Me!

Preaching in the
Year of Matthew

Good News!

Preaching in the
Year of Mark